George Washington

1st President

Born: February 22, 1732
Birthplace: Pope's Creek,
        Westmoreland County,
        Virginia
Political Party: Federalist
State Represented: Virginia
Term: April 30, 1789–March 3, 1797
Died: December 14, 1799
Vice President: John Adams (F)

George Washington was a fourth generation American. He was raised on the family plantation. He had only seven or eight years of education. He was very good in math and became a surveyor by the age of fifteen. He was a leader in the French and Indian War, a gentleman farmer and a state legislator. He became angry about regulations Britain was enforcing and spoke out against them. He participated in the first Continental Congress and was elected Commander in Chief of the second. He led American troops for seven years before the British surrendered. Five years after the war, he was president of the Constitutional Convention. Once the Constitution was approved, he was elected president. Words spoken at his funeral sum up how the nation felt about him: "First in war, first in peace, and first in the hearts of his countrymen."

DISCOVER FOR YOURSELF

Fill in the answer to each clue on the lines to the right.

Brother who cared for Washington after father died
  __ __ __ __ __ __ __ __
   1 2 3 4 5 6 7 8

Where Washington was inaugurated
  __ __ __ __ __ __ __
   9 10 11 12 13 14 15

From whom Washington wanted to gain independence
  __ __ __ __ __ __ __
  16 17 18 19 20 21 22

Where capitol moved during Washington's terms
  __ __ __ __ __ __ __ __ __ __ __ __
  23 24 25 26 27 28 29 30 31 32 33 34

Body that nominated him for president
  __ __ __ __ __ __ __ __
  35 36 37 38 39 40 41 42

Fill in the letters whose number matches those under the lines below to learn what General spoke at Washington's funeral.

"__ __ __ __ __   __ __ __ __ __   __ __ __ __ __"   __ __ __
 22 5 37 17 12   26 18 38 24 19   32 13 4 21 29   1 10 40

...AND AT THE SAME TIME

What did Eli Whitney develop during Washington's presidency? _____

John Adams

2nd President

Born: October 30, 1735
Birthplace: Braintree, (later Quincy),
            Massachusetts
Political Party: Federalist
State Represented: Massachusetts
Term: March 4, 1797–March 3, 1801
Died: July 4, 1826
Vice President: Thomas Jefferson
              Democratic-Republican

Name _____

John Adams was the eldest son of a farmer, John Adams, and Susanna Boylston, of a leading Massachusetts family. He was a Harvard graduate. He taught school briefly before practicing law. Adams was a leader against British colonial policies. He relished every act of opposition toward the British, and yet his high principles led him to defend British soldiers for their part in the Boston Massacre. As a delegate to the Continental Congress he was an advocate of independence. He was on the committee that wrote the Declaration of Independence. His most successful act as a diplomat was having The Netherlands recognize American sovereignty. He felt the vice presidency was an "insignificant office". He was president during a controversial time, but kept the country out of war. Adams could be blunt, impatient and vain, but he had strong convictions which in time have been proven right.

DISCOVER FOR YOURSELF

Circle the hidden words in the puzzle that answer the clues below. Answers appear forward, backward, down or diagonally. Write the answer to each clue on the line next to or under it.

Wife's first name _____

Two men that negotiated Treaty of Paris

with him _____

Adams' age at death _____

A British law passed in 1765 that levied

higher taxes _____

```
J  A  Y  T  E  N  I  N
A  Y  A  H  R  E  I  E
C  A  B  I  A  L  G  E
T  N  I  L  K  N  A  R
T  I  G  N  I  T  Y  H
S  T  A  M  P  A  C  T
I  R  I  G  A  I  L  A
F  R  L  I  N  I  N  E
```

. . . AND AT THE SAME TIME

A German composer that lived during Adams' time and was going deaf. _____

Thomas Jefferson

Name _____

3rd President

THE LOUISIANA PURCHASE

Born: April 13, 1743
Birthplace: Shadwell, Virginia
Political Party: Democratic-Republican
State Represented: Virginia
Term: March 4, 1801–March 3, 1809
Died: July 4, 1826
Vice President: Aaron Burr (DR)
                      George Clinton (DR)

Thomas Jefferson came from a family that valued education. Much of his early learning was with private tutors. He became head of the family at fourteen when his father died. After two years of college he studied law. Not only was he talented as a lawyer, but he was also skilled as an architect, inventor, farmer and musician. He was the main author of the Declaration of Independence. He felt strongly about the fight for freedom, but he had no desire to be a soldier. He felt more useful as a lawmaker. He was responsible for land reforms and the Bill of Rights. He fought for the common man and was a proponent of states' rights. His principles conflicted with the federalists. He formed the Democratic-Republican Party. The Louisiana Purchase and Lewis and Clark's Expedition were his biggest accomplishments as president—and important and lasting today.

DISCOVER FOR YOURSELF

Write the answer to each clue in the row of boxes to the right. Rearrange the circled letters on the lines below to name one of Jefferson's inventions.

His favorite hostess

He was minister to this country

Where Lewis and Clark explored

Name of his estate

His vice president tried for treason

What Jefferson invented _____

...AND AT THE SAME TIME

What was the name of the steamboat that made the first successful trip between

New York City and Albany, and who was on it? _____

James Madison

4th President

Born: March 16, 1751
Birthplace: Port Conway, Virginia
Political Party: Democratic-Republican
State Represented: Virginia
Term: March 4, 1809–March 3, 1817
Died: June 28, 1836
Vice President: George Clinton (DR)
              Elbridge Gerry (DR)

Name _____

James Madison was a sickly child, the oldest of twelve. He received his early education from his parents, tutors and a private school. After he graduated from the College of New Jersey (now Princeton), he studied for the ministry but soon turned to politics. He served in Virginia's legislature, the Continental Congress, the Constitutional Convention, the senate and in Jefferson's administration as secretary of state before becoming president. Madison tried to stay out of war, but finally declared it June 18, 1812. After three years the war ended with no "winner". Madison was able to spend time directing the government in the national interest. The title, "Father of the Constitution" certainly belongs to Madison. Not only was he the primary author, but he defended and practiced it throughout his political career.

DISCOVER FOR YOURSELF

Write the answers to each clue or question in the row of boxes following. The number in the boxes where the letter **E** falls will add up to the number of states in the Union at the end of Madison's presidency.

The name of Madison's home

1	5	2	8	2	3	7	4	4	6

A book on political theory written by Madison and Alexander Hamilton and John Jay

2	3	1

6	1	5	2	1	4	3	7	8	3

After the battle against what fort was the Star-Spangled Banner written?

2	1	3	6	1	2	4

Madison was called this nickname by his friends

4	2	1	1	6

Number of states in the Union _____

. . . AND AT THE SAME TIME

How are J.J. Audubon, Charles Wilson Peale and Jonathan Trumbull alike? _____

James Monroe

MONROE DOCTRINE

5th President

Born: April 28, 1758
Birthplace: Westmoreland County,
           Virginia
Political Party: Democratic-Republican
State Represented: Virginia
Term: March 4, 1817–March 3, 1825
Died: July 4, 1831
Vice President: Daniel Tompkins (DR)

James Monroe was the son of a planter. After a tutorial and private school education he went to the College of William and Mary. He left there after only a few months to join the army and fight in the Revolutionary War. After service he studied law with Jefferson who became his lifelong friend and advisor. As a politician he served in several state and national offices and in the administrations of Washington, Jefferson and Madison. Monroe was an aggressive statesman. He spoke his views. He was the main person responsible for negotiating the Louisiana Purchase. Monroe was popular as president. He was especially strong in foreign affairs. During his administration the United States obtained Florida, settled on the Canadian border and Oregon's occupation. His greatest accomplishment "The Monroe Doctrine" is the basis of our foreign policy today.

DISCOVER FOR YOURSELF

Write the answer to each clue in the row of boxes to the right.

What is the surprise vertical word? _____

President for whom Monroe was Secretary of State?

Person with a strong love for his country

Settlers in America

Number of states or part of states involved in the Louisiana Purchase?

Two states involved in a compromise (5, 6)

1.
2.
3.
4.
5.
6.

. . . AND AT THE SAME TIME

From where and to where did the Savannah sail? _____

John Quincy Adams

Name _____

6th President

Born: July 11, 1767
Birthplace: Braintree,
          Massachusetts
Political Party: Democratic-
          Republican
State Represented: Massachusetts
Term: March 4, 1825–March 3,
          1829
Died: February 23, 1848
Vice President: John Caldwell
          Calhoun (DR)

John Quincy Adams was a precocious child. He attended private schools in America and abroad when he traveled with his diplomat-father. He graduated from Harvard, became a lawyer, and wrote about politics. He served as a diplomat in Europe for three presidents. Through his childhood associations he became a linguist and well informed on many subjects. He was a capable secretary of state under Monroe. In fact, Adams was responsible for many of Monroe's foreign accomplishments. He held several elected offices, but his independent actions separated him from his party. He barely won the presidency. The House of Representatives elected him because he did not have a plurality. He lost his bid for a second term, but he became a representative in Congress where he argued strongly for what he believed, no matter how controversial. In fact, he had a stroke debating an issue and died two days later.

DISCOVER FOR YOURSELF

Across
1. First party to which J.Q. Adams belonged
3. His home
5. Name of treaty signed after War of 1812
7. Last party to which he belonged
8. The man who received more electoral votes in 1824

Down
1. Number of children
2. Institution he established; still in Washington, D.C.
4. The man who made it possible to win the presidency in 1824
6. Wife's name

. . .AND AT THE SAME TIME
What did Hans Oersted discover around 1820? _____

Andrew Jackson

"Our Federal Union : it must be preserved."

7th President

Andrew Jackson was the first president born in a log cabin. He had no male adult to look up to as his father died before he was born. Jackson was self-made. He went to school until he was thirteen. Then he fought in the Revolutionary War. The scar on his forehead came when he refused to obey his captors. He had a reputation of being tough and was nicknamed "Old Hickory". In spite of his limited education, he became a lawyer and politician in what was to be Tennessee. He became a national hero in the War of 1812. His military fame helped him win the presidency. He was the first president to be elected by the people. Opponents dubbed his supporters "the mob". He was a strong leader. He used the powers of the presidency to veto and argue with Congress for the benefit of the working man. He fought for the preservation of the Union.

Born: March 15, 1767
Birthplace: Waxhaw District, South Carolina
Political Party: Democratic
State Represented: Tennessee
Term: March 4, 1829–March 3, 1837
Died: June 8, 1845
Vice President: John Calhoun (D)
Martin Van Buren (D)

DISCOVER FOR YOURSELF

Find the letters that spell the names of the four Indian tribes that were moved west of the Mississippi. Cross them out as you write them in the lines below.

_____

_____

Find the letters that spell the name of the one tribe that did not move. Write its name on the line below.

_____

The letters that remain will spell Jackson's slogan. Unscramble the letters and write his slogan. (4 words) _____

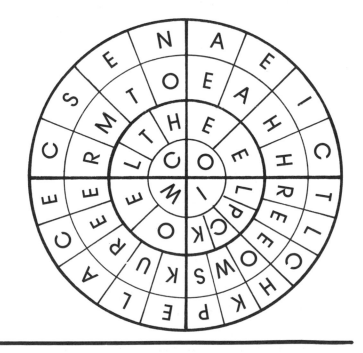

. . . AND AT THE SAME TIME

What did Michael Faraday discover? _____

 IF8750 U.S. Government

Martin Van Buren

Name _____

8th President

Born: December 5, 1782
Birthplace: Kinderhook, New York
Political Party: Democratic
State Represented: New York
Term: March 4, 1837–March 3, 1841
Died: July 24; 1862
Vice President: Richard Johnson (D)

Martin Van Buren was the son of a truck farmer-innkeeper father. He met politicians who stopped by the inn on their way to and from the state capital. He became a law clerk at age fourteen after attending a village school. By twenty-one he had a successful law practice. He was ambitious as a politician. He was nicknamed "Little Magician" because of his political prowess and his small size. Helped Andrew Jackson win the presidency, and as a reward Jackson appointed him secretary of state and then vice president. In 1836, Van Buren was elected president. Soon after, the nation suffered a depression. Van Buren's popularity decreased because of the financial panic, border disputes and accusations from pro-slavery and anti-slavery leaders. He was defeated in his bid for a second term and a third time in 1848 when he ran on the Free Soil Party ticket—a group opposed to slavery.

DISCOVER FOR YOURSELF

Fill in the time line with either the date or the event.

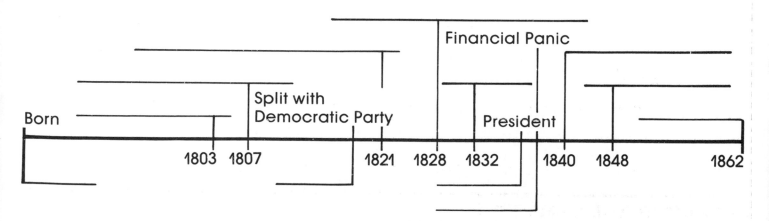

. . . AND AT THE SAME TIME

Who became the monarch of England in 1838 and for how long? _____

William H. Harrison

9th President

Born: February 9, 1773
Birthplace: Berkely, Charles City County,
      Virginia
Political Party: Whig
State Represented: Ohio
Term: March 4, 1841–April 4, 1841
Died: April 4, 1841
Vice President: John Tyler (W)

William Henry Harrison was a descendent of a prominent Virginia family. His early schooling was at home. He left college before graduation to study medicine. When his father died, he joined the army. After seven years of a military career he entered politics. As governor of the Indiana Territory he was victorious against the Indians at the Battle of Tippecanoe, and again showed his military skill in the War of 1812. After that war he resigned again from military life. He ran his farm, was a state and U.S. senator and a diplomat. He was unsuccessful in 1836 in his bid for the presidency, but in 1840 he won on the slogan "Tippecanoe and Tyler too". He caught cold at his inauguration. It turned into pneumonia and he died after only thirty-two days in office. He was not president long enough to put any programs into effect, so it is difficult to say if he was successful as president.

DISCOVER FOR YOURSELF

Mark the following statements true or false.

_____ Harrison never went to college.

_____ Seventy-three electoral votes were enough to win the presidency then.

_____ He received the name Tippecanoe because he had an accident in a boat.

_____ He served as Secretary to the Northwest Territory.

_____ Harrison ran for president more than once.

_____ He served the shortest time in office of any president.

. . . AND AT THE SAME TIME

Charles Dickens was an English author. He wrote many books at this time. Name two of them. _____

John Tyler

10th President

Born: March 29, 1790
Birthplace: Charles City County, Virginia
Political Party: Whig (D/R)*
State Represented: Virginia
Term: April 6, 1841–March 3, 1845
Died: January 18, 1862
Vice President: vacant

Name _____

John Tyler was the son of a distinguished plantation family. He went to private school and William and Mary College. Upon graduation he studied law with his father. He entered politics and held state and national offices. He had been a Democratic-Republican but became a Whig. When Harrison died Tyler found himself without a party because he could not agree with the Whig legislators.* He had opposing views about national banks, tariffs, federally financed projects and slavery. In spite of these differences he passed settlement laws, established trade with China, ended the second Seminole War, and paved the way for Texas' annexation. Above all else, he established the presidency as a full-powered position when reached as a result of the president's death. At the end of the term he retired from politics until 1860 when he voted in favor of Virginia's leaving the Union at the state secession convention.

DISCOVER FOR YOURSELF

Fill in the blanks.

The _____ Party was comprised of several groups with no agreed upon policies.

Tyler _____ many of Congress' bills.

His _____ was his White House hostess until he married _____ _____ , his second wife.

His party disagreements were so strong that some Whigs tried to _____ him.

After fighting with the _____ Indians ended, _____ became a state.

_____ is the name of his estate.

. . .AND AT THE SAME TIME

What did the message Morse tapped out in 1844 say? _____

James K. Polk

11th President

Name _____

James Polk was the eldest of ten children. He was sickly and therefore spared doing his share of farm chores. Although he had little formal education, he was studious and after graduating from the University of North Carolina he studied law. Politics proved more exciting than practicing law, and soon Polk was involved in state and then national politics. He was nominated at the Democratic Presidential Convention on the ninth ballot. He was the first "Dark Horse" candidate to run and then win the presidency. During his tenure America had its largest growth. He guided the nation through the Mexican War and settled the Oregon boundary. He was able to complete the program he outlined during the campaign—something few presidents are able to do. He kept his campaign promise and did not seek a second term.

Born: November 2, 1795
Birthplace: Near Pineville, Mecklenburg County, North Carolina
Political Party: Democratic
State Represented: Tennessee
Term: March 4, 1845–March 3, 1849
Died: June 15, 1849
Vice President: George Dallas (D)

DISCOVER FOR YOURSELF

Fill in the answer to each clue on the lines to the right. Add up the numbers under every letter **A** to discover what Polk's age was when he became president.

The name of his home
‾‾ ‾‾ ‾‾ ‾‾   ‾‾ ‾‾ ‾‾ ‾‾ ‾‾
1　5　2　6　　4　7　9　8　3

A friend of the family and a man Polk supported as president
‾‾ ‾‾ ‾‾ ‾‾ ‾‾ ‾‾ ‾‾
2　5　5　3　6　1　4

Wife's name
‾‾ ‾‾ ‾‾ ‾‾ ‾‾
9　8　2　6　4

His opponent for president
‾‾ ‾‾ ‾‾ ‾‾ ‾‾　‾‾ ‾‾ ‾‾ ‾‾
4　5　7　1　9　　1　5　7　3

Country with whom he settled Oregon boundary
‾‾ ‾‾ ‾‾ ‾‾ ‾‾ ‾‾ ‾‾
1　6　3　4　5　7　2

Original family name
‾‾ ‾‾ ‾‾ ‾‾ ‾‾ ‾‾ ‾‾
8　3　7　4　9　5　6

He was _____ years old when he became president.

. . . AND AT THE SAME TIME

What did William Morton do in 1846? _____

Zachary Taylor

12th President

Born: November 24, 1784
Birthplace: Montebello, Orange County,
      Virginia
Political Party: Whig
State Represented: Louisiana
Term: March 4, 1849–July 9, 1850
Died: July 9, 1850
Vice President: Millard Fillmore (W)

Zachary Taylor was raised near the Kentucky frontier on the family farm. There were no schools, so he studied with tutors. He joined the army in his teens and had a military career for forty years. He fought in many battles and became a hero. The Whig Party recognized his popularity and drafted him as their nominee. He was the first military leader to become president without holding a political office previously. He realized he lacked experience so he sought advice from others, but his decisions were always based on his perception of each situation. Slavery and the extension of slavery in the newly acquired western land were the main issues of his term. They were never resolved however, because he died suddenly after only sixteen months in office.

DISCOVER FOR YOURSELF

What day of the week was Taylor inaugurated? _____

What was his nickname? _____

What was happening in California at the time of Taylor's term? _____

Who was his private secretary and what was the relation? _____

_____

With what country was the Clayton-Bulwer Treaty signed? _____

Why did President Polk send General Scott to lead the army into Mexico rather

than Taylor? _____

...AND AT THE SAME TIME

Who discovered gold first and where in California? _____

Millard Fillmore

13th President

Born: January 7, 1800
Birthplace: Summerhill, Cayuga County,
   New York
Political Party: Whig
State Represented: New York
Term: July 10, 1850–March 3, 1853
Died: March 8, 1874
Vice President: vacant

Millard Fillmore was born in a log cabin. He had a limited elementary school education. When he was fourteen he became an apprentice to a clothmaker until he decided to study law. He was elected to several state offices and to the U.S. House of Representatives. He succeeded to the presidency after Zachary Taylor's death. Fillmore delayed the Civil War with passage of the Compromise of 1850. He worked for the expansion of the U.S. railroads, sent Commodore Matthew C. Perry to Japan to establish trade and diplomatic relations, and reduced the five cent stamp to three cents. The Whig Party was angry about his attitude toward slavery. They did not renominate him. He returned to Buffalo and resumed his law practice. He was nominated in 1856 for president but lost. He lived out his life as a philanthropic citizen in Buffalo.

DISCOVER FOR YOURSELF

The names of the two parties that nominated Millard Fillmore are hidden in the puzzle to the right. Start in the box where the arrow is pointing. Move from letter to letter in any direction without jumping a letter. What are the names of the two parties that nominated him?

_____

_____

	T	N	O	H	I
E	H	W	O	T	N
S	K	N		G	A
E	A	P	I	D	N
I	T	R	G	H	W

. . . AND AT THE SAME TIME

Who was the Emperor of France in 1852? _____

Franklin Pierce

14th President

Born: November 23, 1804
Birthplace: Hillsborough,
　　　　　　New Hampshire
Political Party: Democratic
State Represented: New Hampshire
Term: March 4, 1853–March 3, 1857
Died: October 8, 1869
Vice President: William King (D)

Name _____

Franklin Pierce was the son of a farmer, innkeeper, militia leader and politician. He went to a local school until age eleven. Then he attended private schools and Bowdoin College. He studied law and practiced law between holding elected state and national offices. During the Mexican War he enlisted in the army. After the war he resumed his law practice until he was nominated for president on the forty-ninth ballot. He was the youngest president to take office. He became unpopular with the signing of a bill that allowed Kansas and Nebraska settlers to vote whether they wanted slavery, in his quest for Cuba, and his sponsorship of a southern transcontinental railroad. The Democratic Party rejected him for a second term. He returned to New Hampshire full of bitterness. Even his community scorned him for his views on slavery.

DISCOVER FOR YOURSELF

Write the answer to each clue or question in the row of boxes to the right. Rearrange the circled letters on the line below to tell what the people in Washington called Mrs. Pierce.

What state nominated Pierce for president?

Who was Mrs. Abby Kent Means?

Pierce's presidential opponent

When had Pierce worked for him?

Pierce's home town

What Washington called Mrs. Pierce _____

. . . AND AT THE SAME TIME

What did Johan Lundstrom invent and manufacture in 1855? _____

James Buchanan

Name _____

15th President

Born: April 23, 1791
Birthplace: Cove Gap,
            Pennsylvania
Political Party: Democratic
State Represented: Pennsylvania
Term: March 4, 1857–March 3, 1861
Died: June 1, 1868
Vice President: John Breckinridge (D)

James Buchanan was born in a log cabin. His father ran a store. Buchanan learned arithmetic while helping in the store and Greek and Latin from the pastor. He graduated from college in 1809 and studied law. He had a good law practice and success in business due in part to his early training. After the time he spent as a volunteer soldier in the War of 1812, he spent the rest of his life in public service. Because he was on diplomatic assignments abroad, his feelings about slavery were not known which made him an acceptable candidate for president. In spite of his diplomatic skill, he was not able to mend the wounds made before his administration. Neither the northern or southern party chose him as a candidate in 1860. After Lincoln was elected, but not yet inaugurated, seven states seceded from the Union and set up the Confederate States. Buchanan retired to his house in Pennsylvania, but remained a supporter of the Union.

DISCOVER FOR YOURSELF

Write the answers to each clue in the row of boxes following. The number in the boxes where the letter *A* falls will add up to the number of electoral votes by which Buchanan beat his opponent.

Name of his home _ _ _ _ _ _ _ _ _
                  3 5 4 8 2 9 7 1 6

Name of first state to secede _ _ _ _ _   _ _ _ _ _ _ _ _
                               10 6 7 5 8   1 8 9 7 3 4 5 9

Country where he held first diplomatic assignment _ _ _ _ _ _
                                                   6 1 8 4 1 7

First Confederate State's president _ _ _ _ _ _ _ _ _   _ _ _ _ _
                                     1 7 10 6 9 8 4 5 8   3 8 2 9 6

Man who lost election to him _ _ _ _ _ _ _
                              10 3 7 9 8 5 1

Buchanan's hostess _ _ _ _ _ _ _   _ _ _ _
                    1 7 8 5 9 6 2   4 6 7 3

By how many electoral votes did he win? _____

. . . AND AT THE SAME TIME

Why did the Pony Express last only a year and a half? _____

Abraham Lincoln

Name _____

16th President

Born: February 12, 1809
Birthplace: Hardin County, Kentucky
Political Party: Republican
State Represented: Illinois
Term: March 4, 1861–April 15, 1865
Died: April 15, 1865
Vice President: (1) Hannibal Hamlin (R)
                (2) Andrew Johnson (D)

Abraham Lincoln's father, a farmer and carpenter, was unable to read or write. Lincoln was self taught as he had less than a year of formal education. He had many jobs, was postmaster of New Salem, and won a seat in the state legislature before completing his study of law. He rode the circuit on horseback trying cases before entering national politics. As a representative to Congress he was against slavery in new territory, but felt the government should not interfere with it where it already existed. In 1856 he joined the Republican Party, an antislavery coalition. He ran against Stephen Douglas for senate. Although he lost, Lincoln became well-known through their debates. Lincoln inherited a tense situation when he became president. War soon broke out. He was shot a few weeks after the start of his second term and never was able to carry out his postwar policies.

DISCOVER FOR YOURSELF

Name several jobs he held as a young man. _____

In what speech did he say, "malice toward none, with charity for all"?

_____

What battle started the Civil War? _____

Why and when was the Gettysburg Address delivered? _____

What proclamation declared freedom for slaves? _____

This proclamation was the basis for what Amendment to the Constitution? _____

How did Lincoln travel to the White House for his inauguration? _____

On what ticket was he elected the second time? _____

. . .AND AT THE SAME TIME

How were people able to communicate with one another over great distances?

_____

Andrew Johnson

Name _____

17th President

Born: December 29, 1808
Birthplace: Raleigh, North Carolina
Political Party: Democratic
State Represented: Tennessee
Term: April 15, 1865–March 3, 1869
Died: July 31, 1875
Vice President: vacant

Andrew Johnson taught himself to read, but his wife was responsible for most of his education. His father died early, and he worked in the tailoring profession. He was somewhat successful in business and became active in local and national politics. He favored the common man. He voted independent of his party and the South from where he came. He was the only southern senator to stay in Washington after his state seceded. Lincoln chose him as his running mate on the National Union Party's ticket. Upon Lincoln's death, the job of Reconstruction befell Johnson. He offered a pardon to all southerners who were not military leaders or officials and brought the seceded states back into the Union. Radicals disapproved. He was impeached but missed conviction by one vote. He remained active in politics after his presidency, and was applauded when he returned to Washington as a senator.

DISCOVER FOR YOURSELF

Mark the following statements true or false.

_____ Johnson was impeached and convicted by one vote.

_____ Austria occupied Mexico in 1865.

_____ Alaska was purchased from Russia.

_____ Stanton was dismissed for being too radical.

_____ Edwin Stanton was Secretary of State.

_____ The purchase of Alaska was called "Seward's Folly".

_____ Johnson died in the senate.

_____ Dynamite was used in the Civil War.

...AND AT THE SAME TIME

Name a French chemist who discovered diseases come from germs. _____

Ulysses S. Grant

Name _____

18th President

Born: April 27, 1822
Birthplace: Point Pleasant, Ohio
Political Party: Republican
State Represented: Illinois
Term: March 4, 1869–March 3, 1877
Died: July 23, 1885
Vice President: (1) Schuyler Colfax (R)
(2) Henry Wilson (R)

Ulysses Grant did not like helping on his father's farm or tannery. His only real fondness was for horses. After graduation from West Point, he served in the Army for several years. After the Mexican War, he left the service and tried to support his family by farming and in business, but he was a failure. He rejoined the Army when the Civil War began. He was put in charge of the Union armies. At the end of the war he was a hero in the North, and the South appreciated his treatment of General Lee. Grant had never associated with a political party, but he seemed to favor the Republicans. They nominated him for president, and he won easily. Some of his appointees were not honest. His able military leadership did not carry over to the presidency. In fact, his family might have been penniless had he not finished his autobiography a few days before he died.

DISCOVER FOR YOURSELF

Write the answer to each clue in the row of boxes to the right. Rearrange the circled letters on the lines below to tell the name of the cabin he built near St. Louis.

A confederate warship

Grant's real first name

Where he first lived with his wife

Some people called him this because he had so many casualties in the war

His wife's name

The name of the cabin near St. Louis was _____

. . . AND AT THE SAME TIME

What happened in Promontory, Utah on May 10th 1869? _____

Rutherford Hayes

Name _____

19th President

Born: October 4, 1822
Birthplace: Delaware, Ohio
Political Party: Republican
State Represented: Ohio
Term: March 4, 1877–March 3, 1881
Died: January 17, 1893
Vice President: William Wheeler (R)

A bachelor uncle served as Rutherford Hayes' guardian because his father died before he was born. Hayes received a good education. He was a successful criminal lawyer until he became a soldier during the Civil War. He was elected to Congress while still fighting, but he would not take his seat until the war ended. After being elected governor of Ohio three times, the Republican Party nominated him for the presidency. The election was close. A special commission had to settle it. Hayes won by one electoral vote. He ended Reconstruction, tried to appoint qualified personnel, and sent troops in where strikers caused riots. He left office at the end of one term as he had promised. He returned to Ohio where he was active in several humanitarian causes until his death.

DISCOVER FOR YOURSELF

The motto by which Hayes lived is hidden in the puzzle to the right. Start in the box where the arrow is pointing. Move from letter to letter in any direction without jumping a letter. Write his motto on the lines below.

	H	A	R	T	E	S	W	H
V	E	E	P	S	Y	B	T	O
E	R	S	I	O	S	E	S	V
T	S	H	R	U	C	I	R	E
S	E	B	Y	T	N	H	S	

_____

_____

_____

. . . AND AT THE SAME TIME

List three inventions of the time. _____

James A. Garfield

20th President

Born: November 19, 1831
Birthplace: Orange, Ohio
Political Party: Republican
State Represented: Ohio
Term: March 4, 1881–September 19, 1881
Died: September 19, 1881
Vice President: Chester Arthur (R)

James Garfield received a good education even though he had to work hard on the family farm and at odd jobs to earn money. He graduated from college, taught and studied law. He fought in the Civil War. He had shown an interest in politics before the war and was elected to the U.S. House of Representatives while still in the Army. He served nine terms in Congress. During this time he was accused of accepting "gifts" illegally, but it was never proven. In 1880, he was nominated for president on the thirty-sixth ballot. As president, he awarded several appointments in return for favors received. A disappointed office seeker shot him. He lived eighty days after the shooting. Because of his death, Congress began immediately to get rid of the "spoils system" and install a civil service system.

DISCOVER FOR YOURSELF

Mark the following statements true or false.

_____ If X-ray had existed, Garfield may have lived.

_____ Garfield's mother saw him inaugurated.

_____ Garfield ran against John Fremont.

_____ He ran on the Half-Breed ticket for president.

_____ Some of Garfield's children served other presidents.

_____ Garfield was very intelligent.

_____ He was shot on July 2, 1881.

_____ He was a sailor as a young man.

_____ He supported Andrew Johnson.

. . .AND AT THE SAME TIME

Clara Barton founded the American Red Cross. What had she done before? _____

Chester A. Arthur

21st President

Born: October 5, 1829
Birthplace: Fairfield, Vermont
Political Party: Republican
State Represented: New York
Term: September 20, 1881–March 3,
        1885
Died: November 18, 1886
Vice President: vacant

Name _____

Chester Arthur attended many local schools because his father's pastoral duties required the family move a lot. After college he studied law and became a defender of civil rights for blacks. He became involved with the start of the Republican Party and accepted political assignments for favors done. He was in the state militia in administrative positions during the Civil War. After the war he returned to practicing law and Republican politics. He was nominated as Garfield's running mate because of his strong party loyalty. Much to the surprise of party leaders, when Arthur succeeded to the presidency, he did not make political appointments. In fact, he signed the Civil Service Act. Arthur knew he had a fatal illness which he kept a secret. After completing the term he retired to New York.

DISCOVER FOR YOURSELF

Circle the hidden words in the puzzle that answer the clues below. Words in the puzzle appear forward, backward or diagonally. Write the answer to each clue on the line next to or under it.

The first skyscraper was
built in this city _____

Wife's name _____

College name _____

His hostess _____

Who the Garfield/
Arthur ticket defeated _____

Branch of service he modernized _____

Number of children he had _____

```
O G A C I H C N
G O N T H R E E
Y T R H A U N D
E L L E N A V Y
N A Y I T H E D
D S O S H S T I
I N E Y A V I K
K C O C N A H S
```

. . .AND AT THE SAME TIME

What was Mark Twain's real name? _____

Grover Cleveland

22nd President – 24th President

Grover Cleveland attended local schools until he was fourteen. Then he had to work to help support the family. He studied law and entered politics as a party worker. He worked his way up through local and state offices. His honesty and hard work earned him the Democratic nomination for president in 1884. A name-calling campaign ensued. Cleveland was the first Democrat elected since the Civil War. He did serve a second term, but not consecutively. He lost in 1888 but was elected four years later. Financial depression and labor problems filled his second term. He was not able to solve all the problems. He did not seek a third term. In his retirement he was a college lecturer and author and eventually regained the respect he had earned.

Born: March 18, 1837
Birthplace: Caldwell, New Jersey
Political Party: Democratic
State Represented: New York
Terms: March 4, 1885–March 3, 1889
           March 4, 1893–March 3, 1897
Died: June 24, 1908
Vice President: (1) Thomas Hendricks (D)
                      (2) Adlai Stevenson (D)

DISCOVER FOR YOURSELF

Fill in the answer to each clue on the lines to the right.

The name he dropped as a boy
$\overline{1}\ \overline{2}\ \overline{3}\ \overline{4}\ \overline{5}\ \overline{6}\ \overline{7}$

What young relatives called him
$\overline{8}\ \overline{9}\ \overline{10}\ \overline{11}\ \overline{12}\quad \overline{13}\ \overline{14}\ \overline{15}\ \overline{16}\ \overline{17}$

What Republicans who supported Cleveland were called
$\overline{18}\ \overline{19}\ \overline{20}\ \overline{21}\ \overline{22}\ \overline{23}\ \overline{24}\ \overline{25}$

The currency of the day $\overline{26}\ \overline{27}\ \overline{28}\ \overline{29}$

Person that defeated him in 1888
$\overline{30}\ \overline{31}\ \overline{32}\ \overline{33}\ \overline{34}\ \overline{35}\ \overline{36}\ \overline{37}$

This VP has a relative in Illinois that is in politics now.
$\overline{38}\ \overline{39}\ \overline{40}\ \overline{41}\ \overline{42}\ \overline{43}\ \overline{44}\ \overline{45}\ \overline{46}$

Cleveland was the only president to marry in the White House. Name his bride.
$\overline{47}\ \overline{48}\ \overline{49}\ \overline{50}\ \overline{51}\ \overline{52}\ \overline{53}\quad \overline{54}\ \overline{55}\ \overline{56}\ \overline{57}\ \overline{58}\ \overline{59}$

Where he lectured
$\overline{60}\ \overline{61}\ \overline{62}\ \overline{63}\ \overline{64}\ \overline{65}\ \overline{66}\ \overline{67}\ \overline{68}$

Fill in the letters whose number matches those under the lines below to learn what he said on his death bed.

$\overline{2}\quad \overline{30}\ \overline{49}\ \overline{41}\ \overline{6}\quad \overline{39}\ \overline{48}\ \overline{34}\ \overline{12}\ \overline{29}\quad \overline{57}\ \overline{45}\quad \overline{5}\ \overline{31}\ \overline{61}\ \overline{29}\quad \overline{39}\ \overline{17}\quad \overline{29}\ \overline{36}\quad \overline{33}\ \overline{62}\ \overline{26}\ \overline{5}\ \overline{39}$

. . .AND AT THE SAME TIME

Why did France give the Statue of Liberty to the U.S.? _____

Benjamin Harrison

Name _____

23rd President

Born: August 20, 1833
Birthplace: North Bend, Ohio
Political Party: Republican
State Represented: Indiana
Term: March 4, 1889–March 3, 1893
Died: March 13, 1901
Vice President: Levi P. Morton (R)

Benjamin Harrison was the descendent of a patriotic family. His early education was with tutors. After college he studied law and became a prominent lawyer. He began to work for the Republican Party. After the Civil War he became interested in holding office. By 1888 he had become known because of his name, and as a soldier, lawyer and politician. The Republicans nominated him for president. He did not win the popular vote, but he did win the electoral vote. He was strong in foreign affairs. He built a two-ocean navy, negotiated trade policies, and created the Pan American Union. He let domestic affairs follow party lines and congressional leadership. His attitude toward taxes, pensions and trusts probably cost him the election in 1892. He practiced law and wrote until his death in his home in Indiana.

DISCOVER FOR YOURSELF

Find the letters that spell the names of the states that joined the Union during Harrison's term. Cross them out as you write them on the lines below.

_____

_____

_____

The letters that remain will spell the name of a campaign song. Unscramble the letters and write the name of the song.
(4 words) _____

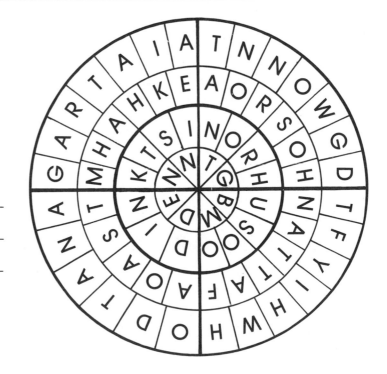

. . .AND AT THE SAME TIME

Where was basketball first played? _____

William McKinley

25th President

Name _____

Born: January 29, 1843
Birthplace: Niles, Ohio
Political Party: Republican
State Represented: Ohio
Term: March 4, 1897–September 14,
    1901
Died: September 14, 1901
Vice President: (1) Garret Hobart (R)
            (2) Theodore Roosevelt (R)

William McKinley went to local and private schools before entering college. After serving in the Civil War he studied law. At an early age he knew he wanted to be president. He held local, state and national offices. He would not travel during the presidential campaign because of his invalid wife, so crowds traveled to hear him speak from his front porch. He had the first popular vote majority since 1872. During his term the Spanish-American War was fought. The U.S. obtained Guam, Puerto Rico and the Philippines in the peace settlement. Domestically he was for higher tariffs and the gold standard. Six months after his second term began, he was shot by an anarchist. He died nine days later.

DISCOVER FOR YOURSELF

Write the answer to each clue in the row of boxes to the right. Rearrange the circled letters on the lines below to tell one of his campaign promises.

Slogan that began the war

Mrs. McKinley suffered with this disease:

The country that gained independence after the Spanish-American War

This man lost to McKinley two times.

The campaign promise he made means they would have this:

Write the promise he made to the voters. _____ _____ _____

. . .AND AT THE SAME TIME

Who discovered the gold in the Klondike? _____

Theodore Roosevelt

Name _____

26th President

Theodore Roosevelt was an energetic yet frail child with a curious mind. He had private tutors until he went to Harvard. Being a lawyer did not interest him but public service did. He was elected to the state legislature at twenty-three. He turned to ranching and writing for a while after his first wife and mother died. He held several appointed offices upon his return to politics. He became a hero as commander of the Rough Riders in the Spanish-American War and was elected governor of New York. The Party did not like the way he ran the state so they ran him for vice president to get rid of him. Six months after the election he was president. Among his many accomplishments was the start of the Panama Canal. He was a conservationist. He was considered a progressive. He did not seek a third term in 1908, but he did run in 1912 and lost. He was involved with politics until the day he died.

Born: October 27, 1858
Birthplace: New York, New York
Political Party: Republican
State Represented: New York
Term: September 14, 1901–March 3, 1909
Died: January 6, 1919
Vice President: (1) vacant
　　　　　　　　 (2) Charles Fairbanks (R)

DISCOVER FOR YOURSELF

Write the answer to each clue in the row of boxes to the right. There will be two words that form vertically. They will be the two missing words from a famous phrase he spoke; "Speak softly and carry a _____ _____ . You will go far."

What Roosevelt won as peace mediator

U.S. Warships that made world tour

Disease he caught in Brazil

Party ticket in 1912

What his kids were called in White House

His home in New York

Group he played tennis with

The president before him

Write the surprise words in the blanks above.

. . . AND AT THE SAME TIME

He wrote <u>Up from Slavery</u> and was an advisor to Roosevelt. _____

William H. Taft

27th President

Name _____

William Taft was a descendant of early settlers in America and a Republican family. He was well educated. He spent twenty years of his life as a judge and practicing law. He held only one elected office before the presidency. All others were appointed. When Roosevelt announced he would not seek another term, he hand-picked Taft. Taft won by over a million votes. He had some Party differences and was not the aggressive administrator Roosevelt had been. Roosevelt did not like the way Taft was handling big business and conservation matters so he decided to run again on the Bull Moose ticket. They both lost. Taft returned to his law practice, wrote, taught and engaged in philanthropic activities until he was appointed as Chief Justice of the Supreme Court in 1921. He finally reached his life's ambition.

Born: September 15, 1857
Birthplace: Cincinnati, Ohio
Political Party: Republican
State Represented: Ohio
Term: March 4, 1909–March 3, 1913
Died: March 8, 1930
Vice President: James Sherman (R)

DISCOVER FOR YOURSELF

Across
4. Custom he established in spring of each year (2 words)
5. President who made him Chief Justice
8. What he said the White House was
9. His Secretary of State

Down
1. Where he was governor
2. Number of electoral votes in 1912
3. Weather on inauguration
6. What Amendment 16 levies (2 words)
7. Brothers and sisters' nickname for him (2 words)

. . . AND AT THE SAME TIME

What two areas were discovered (1909 and 1911) and by whom? _____

Woodrow Wilson

Name _____

28th President

Born: December 29, 1856
Birthplace: Staunton, Virginia
Political Party: Democratic
State Represented: New Jersey
Term: March 4, 1913–March 3, 1921
Died: February 3, 1924
Vice President: Thomas Marshall (D)

Woodrow Wilson's family was a religious one and valued a good education. He was taught at home until he was nine because the war had closed many schools. Wilson studied law but decided he liked teaching. As president of Princeton he emerged as a man for the masses and honest—a perfect candidate for governor of New York. He was a reformer and used the governorship as a stepping stone to the presidency. He won that nomination on the forty-sixth ballot. He won the election because of the split Republican ticket. He fought for the people and aggressively pursued his idealistic views. That, along with keeping the nation out of war, won Wilson a second term. However, three months later the U.S. was at war. After the war, he worked for peace. He suffered a stroke while still in office, but he did not give up the presidency. He died three years after leaving the White House.

DISCOVER FOR YOURSELF

By what name was he called as a child? _____

For what college was he president? _____

What war was being fought when he was a boy? _____

When did he say, "Let the people come forward."? _____

What act did he sign into law that set up the U.S. central banking system

used today? _____

What war was fought during his administration? _____

For what cause was he fighting when he had his stroke? _____

Where is he buried? _____

. . . AND AT THE SAME TIME

What was the Lusitania and what happened to it? _____

Warren G. Harding

Name _____

29th President

Warren Harding attended school, taught, read law and sold insurance before he settled on publishing. Through his journalistic work he became known in the state and was elected to state senator, lieutenant governor and U.S. senator. He worked his way through Party ranks and was nominated for the presidency in 1920. He relied on his cabinet and Congress for leadership. Some of his appointments proved to be corrupt and used their offices for personal gain. When the scams were revealed, cabinet members and friends were sent to jail and committed suicide. In an effort to regain confidence in his administration, Harding made a trip by train across the country. He became ill on the trip and died. The exact cause is not known. His wife burned as many of his papers as she could to protect his name.

Born: November 2, 1865
Birthplace: Corsica, Ohio
Political Party: Republican
State Represented: Ohio
Term: March 4, 1921–August 2, 1923
Died: August 2, 1923
Vice President: Calvin Coolidge (D)

DISCOVER FOR YOURSELF

Fill in the blanks.

The _____ involved leasing government-owned oil reserves to private companies.

_____ was Harding's political sponsor.

Harding brought so many of his friends to Washington, that they were called the _____ .

Harding died in _____ .

The 1920 election was the first time _____ were allowed to vote.

A _____ broadcast the results of the election for the first time in 1920.

When the nominating convention was deadlocked, they nominated Harding as the _____ candidate.

. . . AND AT THE SAME TIME

What automobile manufacturer sold the most cars in 1921? _____

Calvin Coolidge

30th President

Name _____

Calvin Coolidge was educated in public and private schools before entering Amherst College. After college he studied law and soon became active in politics, following in his father's footsteps. He held many local and state offices before being recognized nationally. He was the opposite of outgoing Harding. He earned the name "Silent Sam" because he was a man of few words and seldom smiled. He was the first vice president to attend cabinet meetings. When Harding died, Coolidge was awakened at his father's farm. After dressing, he was sworn in by his father, and then went back to bed. Coolidge cleaned up the scandals of Harding's administration. He was honest and frugal. He won the 1924 election in his own right using the slogan "Keep Cool with Coolidge". He chose not to run in 1928 and said, "Good-bye, I have had a very nice time in Washington."

Born: July 4, 1872
Birthplace: Plymouth, Vermont
Political Party: Republican
State Represented: Massachusetts
Term: August 3, 1923–March 3, 1929
Died: January 5, 1933
Vice President: (1) vacant
              (2) Charles Dawes III (R)

DISCOVER FOR YOURSELF

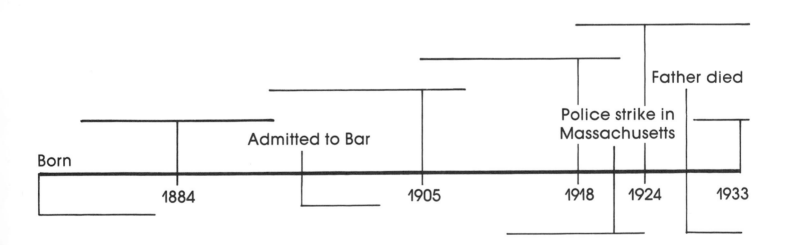

Father died

Police strike in
Massachusetts

Admitted to Bar

Born

1884   1905   1918 1924   1933

. . . AND AT THE SAME TIME

Where were the first Winter Olympics held and in what year?

_____

Herbert C. Hoover

31st President

Name _____

Herbert Hoover's parents were dead by the time he was nine. He was raised by several relatives and had a sporadic early education. His college degree was in geology and mining engineering. He made a fortune developing mines all over the world. He served in the administrations of Wilson, Harding and Coolidge. He was a highly organized administrator as head of the U.S. Food Administration and Secretary of Commerce. His skills were recognized by the Republican Party and he was nominated for president in 1928. He won in a landslide victory, but lost the same way in 1932—probably due to his inability to stop the Depression that hit seven months after he took office. He had many active years after his term as an author, humanitarian and advisor to two presidents. He gave the money he made from the government jobs to charitable projects.

Born: August 10, 1874
Birthplace: West Branch, Iowa
Political Party: Republican
State Represented: California
Term: March 4, 1929–March 3, 1933
Died: October 20, 1964
Vice President: Charles Curtis (R)

DISCOVER FOR YOURSELF

Circle the hidden words in the puzzle that answer the clues below. Answers appear forward, backward, up, down or diagonally. Write the answer to each clue on the line next to or under it.

Where he went to college _____

Troops from this country invaded Manchuria _____

Hoover's 1928 opponent (2 words) _____

Hoover's wife's name (2 words) _____

He was last of this type president.(2 words) _____

Hoover was this by the age of nine _____

K	C	U	D	E	M	A	L
L	A	D	H	M	E	O	I
I	L	R	U	A	U	R	A
E	V	O	O	H	H	P	N
R	L	F	E	C	O	H	E
U	O	N	N	A	P	A	J
R	R	A	J	A	P	N	A
Y	M	T	A	N	F	R	D
A	L	S	M	I	T	H	O

. . . AND AT THE SAME TIME

When were the first Academy Awards held and what was the best film? _____

Franklin D. Roosevelt

Name _____

32nd President

Franklin Roosevelt was born into a wealthy family. He had tutors or went to private schools and traveled in Europe with his family. After Harvard he studied law, but decided politics was what he wanted. He won some and lost some elections, but he was a fighter as was proven when he was struck with polio. He refused to give up and was elected president eleven years later. The words he spoke at his inauguration, "The only thing we have to fear is fear itself" gave the people confidence in his ability to lead them. He led the country through two huge "battles": the Depression and World War II (the end of which he did not see). He had more accomplishments—far too many to list. He was elected to three more terms. No other president ever has or ever will serve that many again. He died about three months after the start of his fourth term.

Born: January 30, 1882
Birthplace: Hyde Park, New York
Political Party: Democratic
State Represented: New York
Term: March 4, 1933–April 12, 1945
Died: April 12, 1945
Vice President: (1) John Garner (D)
                (2) John Garner (D)
                (3) Henry Wallace (D)
                (4) Harry Truman (D)

DISCOVER FOR YOURSELF

Across
1. Man killed in assassination attempt instead of Roosevelt
3. Number of children he had
6. What his "talks" on radio were called (2 words)
8. The event in 1941 that brought U.S. into the war (2 words)
9. World War II actually began when Germany invaded this country in 1939

Down
1. T. Roosevelt and F. Roosevelt were this
2. What the enemy was called
4. What Roosevelt called his program
5. What Franklin Roosevelt was called for short
7. His mother's name

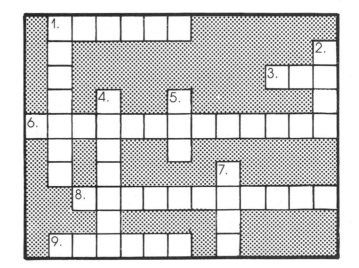

. . . AND AT THE SAME TIME

What was the name of the plane Wiley Post flew around the world? _____

When did he do it? _____

Harry S. Truman

33rd President

Born: May 8, 1884
Birthplace: Lamar, Missouri
Political Party: Democratic
State Represented: Missouri
Term: April 12, 1945–January 20, 1953
Died: December 26, 1972
Vice President: (1) vacant
            (2) Alben Barkley (D)

Name _____

Harry Truman never went to college. He wanted to go to West Point, but his vision was too poor. He joined the state National Guard and served in France during World War I. Before becoming a U.S. senator in 1934, he had several jobs. He was elected with the help of Tom Pendergast, Party boss, but in Washington Truman exposed the Pendergast machine. Truman saved the U.S. millions when he investigated defense spending. His honesty brought him the vice presidential nomination in 1948. Eighty-three days later he was president. The war soon ended in Europe. Truman's decision to drop the atom bomb ended the war in the Pacific. He changed from a wartime to a peacetime economy. He won an upset victory in 1948. He fought against communism, for civil rights, and established NATO during his term. He did not run again, but he did remain active in politics.

DISCOVER FOR YOURSELF

Write the answer to each clue in the row of boxes to the right. There will be two words that form vertically. They will tell two things he did for recreation.

Meeting with Churchill and Stalin in 1945

First Commander of NATO

His program gave rich and poor the same

Armed forces under one department of

Past president hired to improve government efficiency

Struggle between communist and democratic countries (2 words)

Where second bomb fell

Plan that aided war-damaged nations

War U.S. entered in 1950

Two things he liked _____

. . . AND AT THE SAME TIME

What small middle-eastern country gained independence in 1948? _____

Dwight D. Eisenhower

Name _____

34th President

Dwight Eisenhower worked in his father's creamery after high school to help pay his brother's education. Later, he went to West Point. During World War I he trained tank battalions. He had several posts between wars and had an outstanding record in all of them. He was appointed commanding chief of American forces in Europe during World War II. He was a hero after the war and was nominated for president. He won by more than any president before. As a general he had fought to win the war. As president he fought to keep the peace. He won his second term by an even greater majority. In his second term he launched the space program. But all was not peaceful. The Cold War was starting again. Castro took over Cuba, and court-ordered desegregation did not go smoothly. He was not allowed a third term by law. He retired to his farm but remained an adviser to his successors.

Born: October 14, 1890
Birthplace: Denison, Texas
Political Party: Republican
State Represented: New York
Term: January 20, 1953–January 20, 1961
Died: March 28, 1969
Vice President: Richard Nixon (R)

DISCOVER FOR YOURSELF

Write the answer to each clue in the row of boxes to the right. Rearrange the circled letters on the line below to tell what Eisenhower called his domestic program.

President of what college

Number of Cabinet members

Wife's name (2 words)

Name of farm

Soviet Premier at the time

Russia's space shuttle

What Eisenhower called his domestic program _____

...AND AT THE SAME TIME

What pitcher pitched a perfect World Series game in 1956 and for what team did he play? _____

John F. Kennedy

35th President

John Kennedy came from a well-educated, prominent, Irish-American family. After college he enlisted in the Navy. He was commissioned as an ensign and commanded a PT boat. After the war he decided to run for office. His family campaigned for him. He had three terms as a representative in Congress before being elected to the U.S. Senate. He worked for aid to undeveloped countries and to end corruptions in unions. He made a name for himself and actively sought the 1960 presidential nomination four years ahead. He debated against Nixon on TV. His energetic and confident style helped him win. His attractiveness grew in the White House. He was forceful in foreign affairs. He started the Peace Corps. He supported equal rights and medical aid. He was shot after almost three years in office and did not live to see some of his legislation passed.

Born: May 29, 1917
Birthplace: Brookline, Massachusetts
Political Party: Democratic
State Represented: Massachusetts
Term: January 20, 1961–
      November 22, 1963
Died: November 22, 1963
Vice President: Lyndon Johnson (D)

DISCOVER FOR YOURSELF

Kennedy had a gift for speaking. He said many "catchy" things in his inaugural address. He said, "A new generation of Americans were now the leaders of government". He called his program the "New Frontier". Find what Kennedy said in his inaugural address about what you can do for your country in the puzzle to the right. Start where the arrow is pointing. Move from letter to letter in any direction without jumping a letter. Write the quotation on the lines below.

	N	K	A	Y	O	
T	O	S	U	T	U	R
R	W	N	A	O	C	U
Y	T	H	R	Y	O	A
C	C	O	F	O	K	S
A	U	A	D	W	H	Y
D	N	O	N	A	T	R
F	O	Y	T	C	O	N
O	R	Y	O	U	R	U

_____

_____

_____

. . . AND AT THE SAME TIME

How many orbits did the first woman astronaut, Valentina Nikolayeva Tereshkova, make around the earth? _____

Lyndon Johnson

36th President

Name _____

Lyndon Johnson did not like to study but he made good grades. His parents had to encourage him to attend college. He began to take an interest in politics and went to work in Washington. He was in the House of Representatives over ten years. In 1948 and 1954 he was elected to the senate. He was a hard-working, persuasive legislator, but he did not convince the Party to nominate him for president in 1960. Rather he was chosen by Kennedy to be his running mate. Johnson was sworn into the presidency aboard Air Force One after Kennedy's assassination. He worked to hold the nation together and to pass some of Kennedy's legislation. He was elected to a full term in 1964. He pushed through many bills, but he also had problems. He declined to run in 1968 hoping there would be more national unity without him. He retired to his ranch in Texas.

Born: August 27, 1908
Birthplace: Stonewall, Texas
Political Party: Democratic
State Represented: Texas
Term: November 22, 1963–
    January 20, 1969
Died: January 22, 1973
Vice President: (1) vacant
        (2) Hubert Humphrey (D)

DISCOVER FOR YOURSELF

Fill in the blanks.

His reform program was called the _____ .

He developed a long friendship with President _____ .

As the Senate _____ it was his job to see that party members were in the Senate when a vote was taking place.

He was unpopular because of the _____ War.

_____ became the first black cabinet member.

His, his wife's, two daughters' and two beagles' names all had the same _____ . What were they? _____

. . . AND AT THE SAME TIME

Who performed the first human heart transplant in 1967? _____

Richard Nixon

37th President

Born: January 9, 1913
Birthplace: Yorba Linda, California
Political Party: Republican
State Represented: New York
Term: January 20, 1969–August 9, 1974
Died: April 22, 1994
Vice President: (1, 2) Spiro Agnew (R)
          (2) Gerald Ford (R)

Name _____

Richard Nixon was an outstanding student and student body leader. He began his political career almost immediately after being admitted to the bar. He enlisted in the Navy during World War II even though it was against his religion. After the war he served as a U.S. Representative and Senator where he became known for his fight against communists. He was an active vice president, but even then he was accused of misusing political donations. He had his first political defeat against Kennedy and a second for governor of California. However, eight years later he was president. He was successful in foreign affairs, but at home a cloud hung over his administration. His vice president had to resign and so did he. He retired to his California home in hopes time would take care of the hurt he caused the nation. Later, he moved back east and sometimes let his opinions be known.

DISCOVER FOR YOURSELF

Find the letters that spell the answers to each clue. Cross them out in the circle as you write them after each clue. The letters that remain will spell out the name of the scandal during Nixon's term. Unscramble the letters and write the answer on the lines below.

He reduced U.S. forces here _____

Two countries he visited _____

Name of the dog about which he made a speech on TV _____

His secretary of state _____

Agnew's replacement (2 words) _____

The name of the scandal was _____

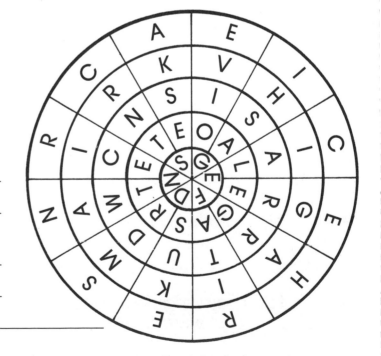

. . . AND AT THE SAME TIME

What words did Neil Armstrong speak when he stepped on the moon? _____

Gerald Ford

Name _____

38th President

Born: July 14, 1913
Birthplace: Omaha, Nebraska
Political Party: Republican
State Represented: Michigan
Term: August 9, 1974–January 20, 1977
Died:
Vice President: Nelson Rockefeller (R)

Gerald Ford was a good student. He studied hard and played football in high school and college. When he received his law degree, he joined the Navy. After the war he resumed his law practice. His family had always encouraged him to accept civic responsibility. He ran for the representative seat in Congress and won—the first of thirteen terms. Ford was popular among his peers, and he was influential as the minority whip. He was nominated and approved vice president after Agnew's resignation. Eight months later, he became president when Nixon resigned. The Democrat-controlled Congress and Ford had differences regarding the economy. Ford vetoed over fifty bills. He pardoned Nixon. In spite of Ford's friendly manner and strong efforts to unify the nation, the public was not consoled. He lost his bid for the presidency in 1976.

DISCOVER FOR YOURSELF

If the answers to the clues are correct, the first letters down will spell two words.

What are they? _____

Town where Ford grew up (2 words)   ___ _____

His Boy Scout rank (2 words)   ___ _____

Republican nominee in 1976   ___ _____

What Ford granted draft dodgers   ___ _____

Name he was born (4 words)   ___ _____

Justice he tried to impeach   ___ _____

Job he had at Yale (2 words)   ___ _____

Man he wrote about in 1976   ___ _____

His running mate (2 words)   ___ _____

Senator he telecast with   ___ _____

. . . AND AT THE SAME TIME

What was the Bicentennial? _____

James E. Carter, Jr.

Name _____

39th President

Born: October 1, 1924
Birthplace: Plains, Georgia
Political Party: Democratic
State Represented: Georgia
Term: January 20, 1977–January 20, 1981
Died:
Vice President: Walter Mondale (D)

Jimmy Carter was an able student and enterprising businessman at age five when he sold peanuts. He went to the U.S. Naval Academy and was in the submarine program when his father died. He resigned from the Navy to run the family business. He was active in civic affairs, always defending those whose rights were being violated. He succeeded in becoming a state senator and governor against all odds. He authored social and moral reforms. He sought the Democratic nomination. Little known outside Georgia, he won support from the voters with his call for a return of honest government. He tried to rid the nation of economic problems, but failed. He achieved more for human rights and world peace. The public's disappointment in his inability to combat financial problems and obtain release of American hostages in Iran probably contributed to his defeat.

DISCOVER FOR YOURSELF

What was Carter's full name? _____

What was the family business? _____

Approximately, by how many popular votes did Carter beat Ford? _____

How many states did Ford win? _____ Carter win? _____

How many electoral votes did Carter win in 1976? _____ In 1980? _____

When were the Iranian hostages freed? _____

Between what two countries did Carter make peace? _____

In what part of the government had his mother been a volunteer? _____

. . .AND AT THE SAME TIME

What is Three Mile Island? _____ What happened there in 1979? _____

_____

Ronald Reagan

40th President

Born: February 6, 1911
Birthplace: Tampico, Illinois
Political Party: Republican
State Represented: California
Term: January 20, 1981–January 20, 1989
Died:
Vice President: George Bush (R)

Name _____

Ronald Reagan did not come from a wealthy background. He worked to help pay for his college education. He acted in school plays and was a student leader. After college he was a sportscaster before entering movies. Reagan was active in politics as a Democrat in 1948, but he became a Republican in 1962. His first public office was governor of California. He tried two times unsuccessfully to run for president before being nominated in 1980. Once elected, he set out to stop inflation, stimulate business and strengthen military defense. His critics cried loud, and his supporters defended him. He won a second term even more convincingly than the first. Terrorism rose worldwide, especially against the U.S. Reagan had proof Libya was behind much of it and ordered Libya attacked. There was criticism from around the world, but Americans stood firm behind their leader.

DISCOVER FOR YOURSELF

Write the answer to each clue in the row of boxes to the right. A word will form vertically. It will be a comet seen in the sky in 1986.

The city where the baseball team was for which he was a sportscaster

The candidate of the Independent Party ticket in 1976

State where he went to high school

One college major

Reagan's mother's name

Age when inaugurated

Other college major

The name of the comet is _____ .

. . .AND AT THE SAME TIME

Who was the first citizen carried into space on January 28, 1986, and what

happened? _____

George Bush

41st President

Born: June 12, 1924
Birthplace: Milton, Massachusetts
Political Party: Republican
State Represented: Texas
Term: January 20, 1989 –
        January 20, 1993
Died:
Vice President: Dan Quayle (R)

George Bush attended grade school in Greenwich, Connecticut, and high school in Andover, Massachusetts. Before completing his degree in economics at Yale University, Bush spent over two years as a Navy pilot during World War II, and won the Distinguished Flying Cross for heroism. After working in the oil industry, Bush became active in Republican politics. Defeated in 1964 for a seat in the U.S. Senate, Bush later became the first Republican to represent Houston in the House of Representatives. He was reelected in 1968 without opposition. Under President Nixon he served as U.S. ambassador to the United Nations, chairman of the Republican National Committee, representative to China, and director of the CIA. In 1980, he lost to Ronald Reagan in the presidential primaries. Reagan then offered him the vice-presidential nomination and Bush readily accepted. After two successful terms as Vice President, Bush was elected our 41st President.

DISCOVER FOR YOURSELF

What job did Bush hold before entering politics? _____

How many hours did Bush serve as acting-President for Reagan? _____

Which Vice President did Bush succeed? _____

What is the name of Bush's wife? _____

To what country was Bush a liaison? _____

Bush's father held what political office? _____

Who was Bush's presidential opponent in 1988? _____

...AND AT THE SAME TIME

Which one of Neptune's moons did Voyager II take photos of? _____

William Clinton

42nd President

Born: August 19, 1946
Birthplace: Hope, Arkansas
Political Party: Democratic
State Represented: Arkansas
Term: January 20, 1993 –
Died:
Vice President: Al Gore (D)

Bill Clinton was born in Hope, Arkansas, and named William Jefferson Blythe IV. As a teenager, he took his stepfather's name, Clinton. He graduated from Georgetown University and Yale Law School. He also spent two years at Oxford on a Rhodes scholarship. Clinton returned to Arkansas to teach law and enter public service. He was elected attorney general for the state of Arkansas in 1976 and became the governor two years later. Clinton lost his bid for re-election in 1980, but became governor again in 1982. He remained in that position until being elected President. Three issues of great interest and concern to him as governor were employment, health care and education. He has promised to continue his efforts in these areas as President. Clinton believes that the federal government should be more responsive to the needs of middle-class, working-class and poor Americans.

DISCOVER FOR YOURSELF

How many years did Clinton serve as Arkansas' governor? _____

Name the president who served as an inspiration to Clinton while Clinton was in high school. _____

What was Clinton criticized for avoiding when he was a young man?

_____

What are the two sports Clinton engages in for relaxation and exercise?

_____ _____

Name the musical instrument Clinton enjoys playing. _____

At the inaugural ceremony, what well-known personality recited a poem she had been asked to compose especially for the occasion? _____

. . . AND AT THE SAME TIME

Name the infamous leader of Iraq at the time Bill Clinton assumed office.

_____

Vocabulary

Name _____

Write the number of the word on the left next to its definition on the right.

1. Electoral College

2. Plurality

3. Diplomat

4. Whip

5. Spoils system

6. Doctrine

7. Domestic

8. Gerrymandering

9. Mugwump

10. Primary

11. Levy

12. Lame duck

13. Caucus

14. Veto

15. Cabinet

16. Speaker

17. Elector

18. "Kitchen" Cabinet

19. Delegate

20. Dark horse

_____ a statement of government policy

_____ collection of money set by the government, a tax

_____ an independent politician; in 1884, one who left the Republican Party

_____ a group of electors that elect the president and vice president of the U.S.

_____ carried on in one's own country

_____ dividing lines of districts to give one political party the advantage

_____ person who handles affairs tactfully without causing ill feeling

_____ power to forbid the carrying out of a project

_____ majority of votes cast for one candidate over all others

_____ the officer in charge of a legislative body

_____ unofficial advisers to the president who may be more important than the official group

_____ one qualified vote

_____ a closed meeting in which decisions are made

_____ member of legislature appointed by party to enforce discipline and attendance during important sessions

_____ an elected office holder continuing in office after defeat before the inauguration of a successor

_____ a little known contestant for a political office

_____ appointments made in exchange for favors rendered

_____ an election where voters nominate their preferred party candidates (or delegates)

_____ a person acting for another, a representative at a convention

_____ a group of advisers to the president

How to Become a Candidate for President Name _____

Many people from either party may want to be president. They can declare themselves as candidates and spend months campaigning before they even win their party's nomination. Once they are the party's candidate, they campaign against the other major candidate until election day.

Mark the following statements true or false.

____ In order to be president a person must be over thirty-five.

____ The two major parties use primaries and national conventions to select their candidates.

____ Women are not allowed to run for president.

____ A party platform is written at each national convention.

____ A candidate for office always says the right thing to all people.

____ What candidates do and say is news.

____ Small party candidates are selected at the conventions.

____ In order to be president a person must be a naturalized citizen.

____ Primaries are held in every state.

____ All delegates to the national conventions have been chosen by the voters.

____ Primary elections select the president.

____ New Hampshire holds the first primary.

____ The two major parties hold their conventions every four years in the summer.

____ The national conventions choose the presidential and vice presidential candidates.

____ Delegates are chosen to go to the national conventions in the primaries.

____ A favorite son is the candidate chosen by the convention.

____ The candidate chosen by the party decides what the party platform will be.

____ When voters choose a delegate, they are actually voting for the candidate of their choice.

____ The vice presidential candidate selected at a national convention is the same party as the presidential candidate.

____ No small party candidate has ever won the presidency.

____ The presidential candidate may choose the vice presidential candidate without the party's approval.

____ When campaigning to be the party's choice as the nominee, a person may spend years.

____ When campaigning to be the people's choice for president, a person has only a little over two months to campaign.

The President's Residence

Name _____

The White House in Washington D.C. is the official residence of the president of the United States. It stands on the site selected by George Washington in 1791. The executive mansion contains the living quarters and offices for the president and his family. The White House has undergone many changes and reconstruction in its nearly 200 year history. Originally there was no plumbing or electricity. Over the years modern conveniences have come to the White House.

Write the answer to each clue in the row of boxes to the right. Two words that will form vertically is what the White House was called originally.

The room where reporters gather

What Dolly Madison saved of Washington

The largest room in the White House

President in 1814

The floor the public may visit

First White House resident

The street White House faces

Entrance where dignitaries enter

Number of rooms

Number of rooms when first lived in

Original architect

President who brought in first stove

What British did to White House in 1814

Floor where oval office is

President when Bell demonstrated phone

What was the White House called originally? _____

The Presidency

Name _____

As the chief executive of the United States, the President helps shape and enforce laws, directs foreign policy, is responsible for national defense, presides at ceremonial affairs, and leads his Party. He does not control the Legislative and Judicial Branches, but he can influence law making, and he does appoint justices to the Supreme Court. No one man can assume all the duties of the president, and so he appoints assistants. They form the White House Office. It is their job to keep the President informed about the many departments of the government. They may advise and influence the president in his decisions. The members of the White House office do not need congressional approval, nor must they answer to the Congress. The Cabinet, consisting of thirteen department heads called secretaries, is also appointed by the President to advise and assist him. However, Cabinet members must be approved by Congress and must answer to the Legislative Branch whenever asked.

Label the diagram below to show the various departments and officials running the government. Use the words from the word box to complete the diagram.

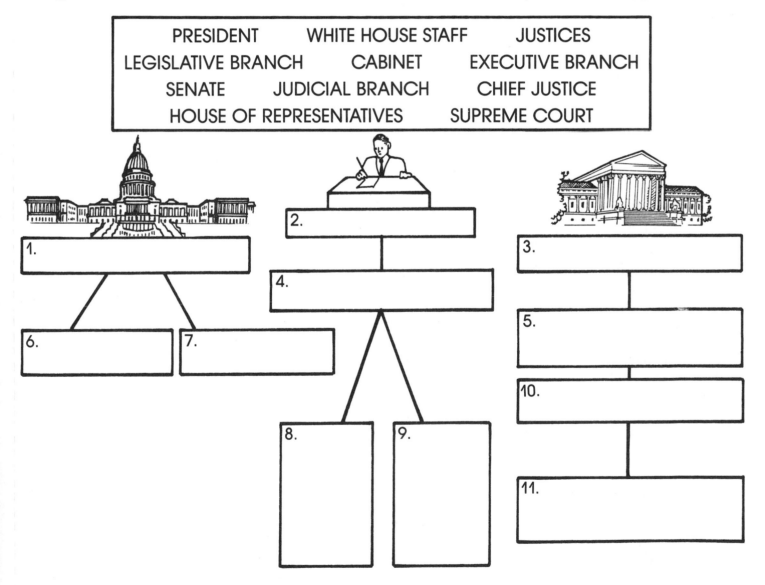

PRESIDENT	WHITE HOUSE STAFF	JUSTICES
LEGISLATIVE BRANCH	CABINET	EXECUTIVE BRANCH
SENATE	JUDICIAL BRANCH	CHIEF JUSTICE
HOUSE OF REPRESENTATIVES	SUPREME COURT

1.

2.

3.

4.

5.

6.

7.

8.

9.

10.

11.

The Presidential Helpers

Name _____

You have learned the president has many assistants. Write the number of the White House Office division on the left of the line to its abbreviated definition on the right.

1. Council of Economic Affairs

2. Council on Environmental Quality

3. Council of Wage and Price Stability
4. Domestic Policy Staff
5. National Security Council

6. Office of Administration
7. Office of Management and Budget
8. Office of Science and Technology Policy
9. Office of the Special Representative for Trade Negotiations
10. Office of the Vice President
11. Intelligence Oversight Board

12. National Productivity Council

____ runs the White House Office, like an office manager

____ provides support to the President however needed

____ studies national economy

____ controls security

____ studies economic trends, may offer advise for controls

____ helps formulate domestic policy

____ studies national environment

____ improves productivity in private industry and government

____ works to increase trade with foreign countries

____ advises on budgetary matters

____ reports on activities of security agencies

____ advises of scientific and technological matters

There are others such as the president's physician, military aides and social secretaries that help the personal life of the presidential family run smoothly that have not been included for definition. They speak for themselves.

The White House Office often works with the Cabinet. List the thirteen departments of the cabinet and the current directors or secretaries.

1. _____
2. _____
3. _____
4. _____
5. _____
6. _____

7. _____
8. _____
9. _____
10. _____
11. _____
12. _____

13. _____

Two Specific Powers

Name _____

Veto

Before a bill passed by Congress can be enacted as law, it must be signed by the President. Therefore, when Congress passes a bill, it sends it to him. The President has several options. He may sign it into law. He may let the bill sit on his desk for ten days, and it will become law automatically. Or, he may veto it. That is, not sign it, but return it to Congress with his objections. The President may not veto just a part of a bill. He returns the entire bill to Congress with his objections. Congress will then try to rework it or they may override the President's veto with a two-thirds veto of their own.

Fill in the blanks.

_____ holds the record for the greatest number of bills vetoed, but was in office longer than any other president. He vetoed 635 bills. The seventeenth president, _____ , had the largest number of vetoes overridden by Congress—15. Make a guess as to how many presidential vetoes there have been since the time of Washington. _____

Impeachment

The Constitution reads, "The President, Vice President, and all Officers of the United States shall be removed from Office on Impeachment for and conviction of Treason, Bribery, or other high crimes or misdemeanors." Impeach means to accuse. Only when an official is tried and found guilty is the official removed from office. One president has been impeached and two were close to impeachment. Can you name them from the clues?

Fill in the blanks.

This president was charged with serious misconduct in office and tried by the Senate. The trial lasted over two months, but he was acquitted by one vote. His name was _____ .

A resolution was introduced to the House to impeach this president, but the resolution was voted down, and the president remained in office. Name him.

_____

The Judiciary committee of the House recommended three articles of impeachment to the full House on this president. However, before any action could be taken, this president resigned rather than face impeachment proceedings. His name was _____ .

Presidential Power

Name _____

When the president takes the Oath of Office "I do solemnly swear (or affirm) that I will faithfully execute the Office of President of the United States, and will, to the best of my ability, preserve, protect, and defend the Constitution of the United States", he accepts the responsibility of running the nation. With the responsibility comes power which could be misused. However, the authors of the Constitution tried to avoid any misuse and provided for the Legislative, Judicial and Executive Branches to be a check for one another. It has worked most of the time.

Mark the following statements true or false to see how much power the President has.

_____ The President is the Commander in Chief of the Armed Forces.

_____ The President may declare war.

_____ The President has the power to grant reprieves and pardons for offenses against the U.S., except in the case of impeachment.

_____ The President has the power to appoint any official to his Cabinet, a Supreme Court justice or an ambassador without approval from Congress.

_____ The War Powers Act was passed so that Congress and the President act together in declaring any act of hostility.

_____ The President is to keep the Congress informed with State of the Union messages from time to time.

_____ A treaty must receive two-thirds approval from the Senate before it is effective.

_____ The President may recommend legislation.

_____ The President may introduce legislation.

_____ The President may make treaties.

_____ The President must see that the laws are executed.

_____ The President does not need to consult with anyone but his Cabinet when he wants a law passed.

_____ The President must sign legislation in order for it to become law.

_____ Congress passed the National Emergencies Act in 1976 to keep the President's power in check.

_____ If a President does not want a law passed, he throws away the bill when Congress sends it to him.

_____ The President can prevent any bill from becoming law unless Congress passes it over his veto.

_____ The President's Cabinet and Office can pass laws.

_____ The President does what his advisers tell him.

Challenge

Name _____

How good is your memory? Name the presidents in order.

1789-1797 _____	1885-1889 _____
1797-1801 _____	1889-1893 _____
1801-1809 _____	1893-1897 _____
1809-1817 _____	1897-1901 _____
1817-1825 _____	1901-1909 _____
1825-1829 _____	1909-1913 _____
1829-1837 _____	1913-1921 _____
1837-1841 _____	1921-1923 _____
1841-1841 _____	1923-1929 _____
1841-1845 _____	1929-1933 _____
1845-1849 _____	1933-1945 _____
1849-1850 _____	1945-1953 _____
1850-1853 _____	1953-1961 _____
1853-1857 _____	1961-1963 _____
1857-1861 _____	1963-1969 _____
1861-1865 _____	1969-1974 _____
1865-1869 _____	1974-1977 _____
1869-1877 _____	1977-1981 _____
1877-1881 _____	1981-1989 _____
1881-1881 _____	1989-1993 _____
1881-1885 _____	1993- _____

Find these other interesting facts.

Name the nine presidents who did not go to college. _____

_____

Has your state ever sent a president to Washington? _____ If yes, name any
who have come from your state. _____

_____

What profession seems to have been the one most presidents pursued before
becoming president?_____ How many were in that profession?____

Pairing Up

Write the number of the president on the line next to the item it matches.

Events

1. Jefferson	____	Emancipation Proclamation
2. Monroe	____	Watergate
3. Nixon	____	Alaska Purchase
4. Harding	____	Missouri Compromise
5. McKinley	____	Social Security Act
6. Wilson	____	Louisiana Purchase
7. Lincoln	____	World War I
8. Grant	____	Teapot Dome
9. A. Johnson	____	Dred Scott Decision
10. Buchanan	____	Spanish-American War
11. F. Roosevelt	____	Transcontinental railroad complete

Nicknames

1. Nixon	____	King Andrew the Great
2. Reagan	____	Father of His Country
3. Lincoln	____	Old Buck
4. McKinley	____	Dude President
5. Arthur	____	Dutch
6. Washington	____	Father of the Constitution
7. Eisenhower	____	Old Tip
8. Jefferson	____	Sage of Springfield
9. T. Roosevelt	____	Tricky Dicky
10. Madison	____	Father of the Declaration of Independence
12. W. H. Harrison	____	Ike
13. J. Q. Adams	____	Wobbly Willie
14. Buchanan	____	Old Man Eloquent
15. A. Johnson	____	Happy Warrior
16. Jackson	____	Tennessee Tailor

Programs

1. F. Roosevelt	____	Manifest Destiny	5. Kennedy	____	The Fair Deal
2. L. Johnson	____	The New Frontier	6. Polk	____	The Great Society
3. Monroe	____	The New Deal	7. Wilson	____	Era of Good Feeling
4. Truman	____	The New Freedom	8. T. Roosevelt	____	The Square Deal

Presidential Onlys

Name _____

Name the person following each "only" statement.

Only one president was sworn into office on an airplane. _____

Only one president has been issued a patent for an invention. _____

Only one president was inaugurated in two different cities for two different but

consecutive terms. _____ Name the cities. _____

_____

Only one president had a child born in the White House. _____

Only one president held the office of vice president and president without being
elected to either. _____

Only one woman was the mother of one president and the wife of another.

_____

He was the only bachelor president. _____

Only one president served two full terms and yet served fifty-seven days short of
eight years. _____ Why? _____

The cause of death for one president is still a "mystery". _____

He was the only president married in the White House. _____

Only one president was a model. _____

Only one president was born on a holiday. _____ What holiday? _____

Only one president resigned the office of the presidency. _____

Only one president's wife was born outside the U.S. _____

Only one president served as speaker of the house. _____

Only one president served two non-consecutive terms. _____

Only one president was an actor. _____

Only one president weighed less than 100 pounds. _____

Only one president has won a Pulitzer Prize for biography. _____

Only one president married a woman whose last name was the same as his. _____

_____

The only vice president that was not of the same party as the president (except at
time of Civil War)? _____

Presidential Firsts

Name _____

Who was the first . . .

- to be nominated for vice president under the 25th Amendment? _____
- president to be elected when the radio was used to give the results? _____
- president on record to have his picture taken? _____
- president elected west of the Mississippi? _____ What year? _____
- president to appear on television? _____ When? _____
- president to hold regular press conferences? _____
- president to be sworn in by a woman? _____
- president to be nominated by a national convention? _____
- president to wear long pants? _____
- president to be sworn in on January 20th? _____ What year? _____
- woman to run for the vice presidency? _____ What year? _____
   With whom did she run? _____ What Party? _____
- president to live in the White House? _____
- president to visit a foreign country while in office? _____
- president born in a log cabin? _____
- president to drive to inauguration in a car? _____
- president to be sworn in behind bulletproof glass? _____
- president to resign? _____
- president to use the handshake rather than a bow? _____
- mother to see her son sworn in as president? _____
- president inaugurated in Washington? _____
- president to appoint a black cabinet member? _____
- president to ride a train while in office? _____
- president to appoint a woman to his cabinet? _____
- president to watch a liftoff into space firsthand? _____
- president to die in office? _____
- president to marry in office (but not in the White House)? _____

Presidential Quiz

Name _____

What two presidents died on the same day? _____

What is interesting about the date of their deaths? _____

_____

One elector wanted Washington to be the only president elected unanimously. In
    order to keep that record, William Plumer voted against what president? _____

Two sets of three presidents have served within one year. Name them and the
year.

1. _____ _____ _____ _____

2. _____ _____ _____ _____

What president never voted for president until he ran for the office? _____

What presidents were related in the following ways?

    father–son _____   fifth cousins _____

    second cousins _____   grandfather–grandson _____

Which state has sent more presidents to Washington than any other? _____

Which president was the youngest when inaugurated? _____ Oldest? ___

Who delivered the shortest inaugural address? _____

How many words? _____

Who delivered the longest inaugural address? _____

How many words? _____

Which man gave up the presidency to the man he took it from? _____

How many presidents have served partial terms due to death in office? _____

Who were the three successive presidents born in Ohio? _____

_____

Which presidents graduated from West Point? _____

Which presidents signed the Constitution? _____

What three presidents' closest opponents had more popular votes, yet they won?

_____

What two presidents lived to be over ninety? _____

Which presidents' fathers signed the Declaration of Independence? _____

Names - Faces - Places

Name _____

Only one state is named for a president. Which one is it? _____

There are four state capitals named for presidents. Name the capitals and their states. _____   _____

_____   _____

There is one paved highway that goes from coast to coast named after a president. What is the name of the highway? _____

What presidents' heads are on the following coins? (No fair peeking.)

penny _____ nickel _____ dime _____

quarter _____ half dollar _____

What presidents' heads are on the following currency? (No peeking now either.)

$1.00 _____ $50.00 _____

$2.00 _____ $500.00 _____

$5.00 _____ $1000.00 _____

$20.00 _____ $5000.00 _____

$100,000.00 _____

What is Mount Rushmore? Describe it and tell where it is. _____

_____

_____

Tell whose president's home each of the following are and where they are located.

Hyde Park _____   Wheatland _____

Mount Vernon _____   Montpelier _____

Sagamore Hill _____   Hermitage _____

Monticello _____   Sherwood Forest _____

Spiegel Grove _____   The Beeches _____

BEFORE THE CONSTITUTION

Name _____

Most colonists who settled in America during its first 150 years were British. They worked hard and suffered many hardships, but they persevered as they built settlements along the country's east coast from what is now Maine to Georgia. They lived under the rule of the British.

The colonists asked for a larger role in making decisions affecting them, but the British only tightened their control. By the mid 1770's, the British government had imposed heavy taxes and restricted the colonists' freedom.

On June 7, 1776, Richard Henry Lee, a delegate to the Second Continental Congress, presented the idea that the colonies should be free and independent states. As a result of his presentation, a committee was appointed to write the Declaration of Independence.

Circle the names of the thirteen colonies in the puzzle. They may be forward, backward, up, down or diagonal. Write them alphabetically on the lines to the right of the puzzle.

```
S I O N I L L I N O T G N I H S A W
I D A H O R E G O N I N D I A N A E
F L O R I D A D N A L S I E D O H R
P A N I L O R A C H T U O S M R Y I
A I C C O N N E C T I C U T A T O H
I N A N G R I V E R M O N T I H K S
P A L E R I H S P M A H W E N C E A
P V I W M W E N E V A D A S E A N I
I L F J O A D E L A E N T U E R T G
S Y O E N I S N S L K E E H S O U R
S S R R T N I A A H R W X C S L C O
I N N S A I H W S L O Y A A E I K E
S N I E N G A E E N Y O S S N N Y G
S E A Y A R Y W Y R A R H S N A E N
I P V R E I G E O M G K A A E O W J
M W E S T V I R G I N I A M T R S Y
```

_____

_____

_____

_____

_____

_____

_____

_____

_____

_____

_____

_____

_____

_____

LEADING TO THE DECLARATION OF INDEPENDENCE

A series of events led to the writing of the Declaration of Independence. Ten years before it was written, America asked the King of England to allow it to have a more active part in making the laws that governed the nation. Their request was denied. England not only continued to make the laws, but they levied more and higher taxes. The Stamp Act required the colonists to pay taxes on legal and business papers. England also taxed many imported goods including tea. The Boston Tea Party protested the tax on tea. All but one colony agreed not to trade with England during the First Continental Congress, but England did not change its ways. A final request asking England to change was sent to King George III just before the Declaration was written.

Answer the questions and fill in the blanks below to learn which colony did not agree to stop trading with England. Its name will appear down in the boxes.

1. Write the name of the King that levied high taxes.

   □ __ __ __ __ __

2. How many years before the Declaration was written did America ask to be a part of the law making process?

   __ □ __

3. Where was a "party" held?

   __ □ __ __ __ __

4. Goods sent into America from another country are ___.

   __ __ __ __ □ __ __ __

5. With what country did America want to share the lawmaking process?

   __ __ □ __ __ __ __

6. Which Continental Congress voted not to trade with England?

   __ □ __ __ __

7. What act taxed many legal and business papers?

   __ __ □ __ __ __ __ __

What state did not agree to stop trade with England? _____

Name _____

DECLARATION OF INDEPENDENCE

The Declaration of Independence was written after the start of the Revolutionary War. It declared America's freedom from British rule. The Second Continental Congress appointed five men, Thomas Jefferson, John Adams, Benjamin Franklin, Robert Livingston and Roger Sherman, to write it. Jefferson wrote the first draft which was almost perfect. The committee made a few corrections before it was presented to the Continental Congress. A few more corrections were made, but the document is basically the work of Jefferson. Church bells rang to signal the adoption of the Declaration of Independence on July 4, 1776—the birth of our nation.

There are five parts in the Declaration: the Preamble, Statement of Human Rights, Charges Against the King and Parliament, Statement of Separation and the Signatures. Though their main purpose was to state the reasons for separation from England, they also expressed some ideals, such as all men are created equal and entitled to the right to life, liberty and the pursuit of happiness. These ideals are also expressed in the Constitution and are the base today of America's beliefs.

Fill in the puzzle below. The circled letters when unscrambled will tell you how many people signed the Declaration of Independence.

Across
1. The main author
3. A member of the committee that wrote the Declaration

Down
1. The month in which it was completed
2. The parts in the Declaration and the number of people on the committee that wrote it.
4. 177 __ __ __, the year it was completed.

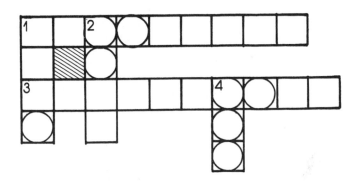

How many signers were there on the Declaration of Independence?

_____

ARTICLES OF CONFEDERATION

During the Revolutionary War the Continental Congress wrote the Articles of Confederation that were meant to form a national government. The Articles are considered the nation's first constitution. Under the Articles the thirteen colonies became thirteen states. The Articles granted each state its independence. The states acted like individual countries. They did not work together. They did not want to give up their individual rights. Under British rule they had, and now each state wanted its own power. The people did not want a strong central government.

The Articles of Confederation set up a Congress of the Confederation. Some states had more members than other states, but each state was allowed only one vote. There was no President, and there were no courts. Congress was limited to what it could do. The states did not have to obey the laws it did pass.

Write **True** or **False** in front of the following statements.

_____ The Articles of Confederation formed a strong central government.

_____ Every state had one vote in Congress no matter what number of delegates represented it.

_____ When Congress asked the states for money to pay national debts, the states did what the Congress asked.

_____ The President ran the Confederation.

_____ Every state did what it wanted.

_____ Every state had the same number of delegates in Congress.

_____ The courts helped make the laws.

_____ The Articles of Confederation was America's first constitution.

_____ Every state had to send men to serve in the army when laws were passed establishing an army.

_____ The President was elected by the Congress.

_____ The Continental Congress wrote the Articles during the Revolutionary War.

_____ The Articles of Confederation worked well.

Name _____

WHY THE CONSTITUTION WAS WRITTEN

Because the thirteen states acted as thirteen separate nations under the Articles of Confederation, the United States was not a unified country, and its government was considered weak. Many leaders of the time recognized the need for a stronger government. Delegates from five states, New York, New Jersey, Virginia, Pennsylvania and Delaware, met in Annapolis in September of 1786 at what is known as the Annapolis Convention. They discussed the trade and boundary problems between states and the states' rights to do as they pleased under the laws of the Articles. From that meeting a recommendation was made that a special convention be held in Philadelphia in 1787 to revise the Articles of Confederation. Delegates from twelve states met in May of 1787. One state refused to send delegates because it was afraid it would lose its individual rights as a state. When the delegates began to discuss ways of correcting the Articles, they realized they would have to write a new document to overcome its faults. And so they worked for four months behind closed doors writing the Constitution.

Answer the questions. Unscramble the circled letters to learn which state did not come to the Constitutional Convention.

What was the name of the convention held in September, 1786?

__ __ Ⓞ __ __ Ⓞ __ Ⓞ __

In what city was the Constitution written?

__ Ⓞ __ __ __ Ⓞ __ Ⓞ __ __ __ __

How long did it take to write the Constitution?

__ __ __ Ⓞ   __ __ __ __ __ Ⓞ

What kind of problems between states did the Annapolis Convention discuss?

__ __ __ __ Ⓞ   Ⓞ __ __   __ __ __ __ Ⓞ __ __ __

What was the name of the state that did not attend the Constitutional Convention?

__ __ __ __ __ __   __ __ __ __ __ __

GETTING STARTED WRITING THE CONSTITUTION

George Washington had won the respect of the delegates as commander of the Revolutionary War Army and was elected President of the Constitutional Convention at its opening on May 25th in Pennsylvania's State House. As President Washington did not make many contributions, but he kept the meetings orderly and running as smoothly as possible considering the many different points of view. Any remarks Washington did make were listened to attentively by the delegates. Before the convention got underway, a rules committee organized the procedures the convention would follow. Each state was given one vote. If there were more than one representative from a state, the delegates would have to decide how to cast their one vote. What happened at the meetings was to be kept secret until the entire Constitution could be presented to the public. Any delegate could voice an opinion. A vote cast one way could be changed if the delegates saw it was necessary as they proceeded.

Complete the crossword puzzle.

Across
1. War Washington commanded army
5. Elected Washington President of convention
7. Where convention took place

Down
2. Means by which different laws settled
3. Month convention began
4. Way in which meetings held
6. Number of votes allowed per state

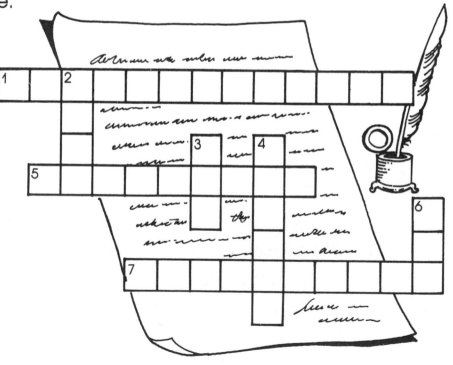

Name _____

THE GREAT COMPROMISE

There were several areas of disagreement. The greatest area was in the matter of how many representatives from each state should be in the legislature. The larger states thought representation should be determined by its population. This was called the Virginia Plan. The states with smaller populations were not in favor of such a plan. They wanted all states to have an equal number of representatives. Their plan was called the New Jersey Plan. Roger Sherman of Connecticut proposed a two house legislature. One, the Senate, would have an equal number of representatives. The other, the House of Representatives, would have a representative for every 30,000 residents. This plan satisfied the large and small states and became known as the Great Compromise.

Circle the answers in the puzzle and write them after each question. The letters that remain uncircled in the puzzle will spell first, the name of Virginia's governor and the name of the man who presented the Virginia Plan, and second, the man who presented the New Jersey Plan.

Which states favored the New Jersey Plan? _____

Representation based on population was which plan? _____

What was the first name of the man proposing the Great Compromise?

_____

What was his last name? _____

Which plan suggested equal representation? _____

Which legislative body has an equal number of representatives? _____

Which states favored the Virginia Plan?

_____

Which man proposed the Virginia Plan? _____

Which man proposed the New Jersey Plan? _____

A	I	N	I	G	R	I	V
E	S	E	D	M	U	R	L
N	H	W	D	R	E	L	A
E	E	J	N	G	A	D	O
T	R	E	O	M	L	P	L
A	M	R	S	H	W	A	I
N	A	S	L	L	R	I	A
E	N	E	M	G	P	A	T
S	E	Y	E	R	S	O	N

THE THREE-FIFTHS COMPROMISE

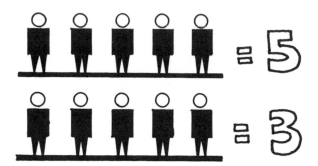

The Northern states were opposed to slavery, and the Southern states were not. The Southern states wanted their slaves counted in the population when it came to the number of congressmen that were allowed in the House of Representatives. They did not want them counted when figuring a state's taxes based on the number of its residents. The Northern states disagreed. The framers of the Constitution never used the words slave or slavery. They suggested that all free persons and three out of five of "all other persons" be counted in the population for the purposes of taxation and representation in Congress. This became known as the Three-fifths Compromise.

Give some thought to the questions below and then write your answers.

What does it mean to compromise? _____

_____

Why were the Southern states willing to count every slave? _____

_____

_____

Why did the North want every slave to be counted? _____

_____

_____

Where was this compromise originally stated in the Constitution?_____

_____

Explain how this compromise worked. _____

_____

_____

_____

Do you think it was a fair compromise? _____ Why or why not? _____

_____

_____

_____

OTHER COMPROMISES

There were other differences between large and small states, believers in a strong central government and states' righters, agricultural and industrial states, and states in different regions. They were all settled by compromise.

A. Whether to tax imported goods became an issue. The Northern states, who were becoming industrial states, wanted taxes placed on imported goods. The Southern states did not because they bought a lot of goods from Europe, including slaves. The compromise reached gave Congress the right to control interstate commerce and foreign trade, but it could not stop slave trade until 1808. A slave owner was taxed for every slave he bought because slaves were considered property.

B. Believers in a strong central government satisfied those who feared it by establishing three branches of government where no one branch could become too powerful. The Constitution provides for each branch to be checked by the other two.

C. The delegates could not decide who should elect the President and Vice President. For this reason an Electoral College was established. Its members were to be appointed by each state legislature, and they in turn cast ballots for the two offices.

Write the letter of the compromise that governs each of the following situations after it.

The person with the most votes becomes President. ____

Foreign goods could be higher priced. ____

The President can veto laws made by Congress. ____

The slave trade ended in 1808. ____

The three branches of government are the Legislative, Executive and Judicial. ____

Taxes on imported goods protected the Northern states. ____

America will never have a king as head of the government. ____

American produced goods could cost less. ____

The Vice President receives the second most votes. ____

The Senate must approve all treaties made by the President. ____

Taxes are not placed on states for exported goods. ____

No one person can make all the nation's laws. ____

Name _____

RECORDING THE EVENTS

James Madison is referred to as the "Father of the Constitution." He was a strong influence in its development. He spoke out more than 150 times and kept a secret record of every session that was not published until after his death.

Make believe that you were present at the time the Great Compromise was settled. Write a diary for the proceedings.

_____
_____
_____
_____
_____
_____
_____

_____
_____
_____
_____
_____
_____
_____

Write an account of how you think the proceedings happened during the debates of how citizens should be counted (the Three-fifths Compromise).

Select one of the other compromises and write about its proceedings.

_____
_____
_____
_____
_____

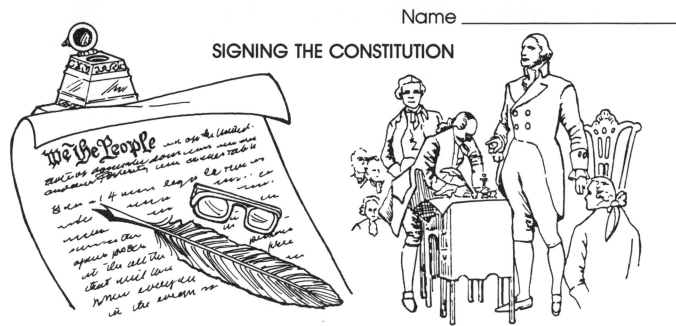

SIGNING THE CONSTITUTION

Only about thirty-five of the delegates were present for most of the entire proceedings. Seldom were all fifty-five there together. The New Hampshire delegates arrived nine weeks late. Other delegates had to leave to take care of business at home. Four delegates, Luther Martin, Robert Yates, John Lansing, Jr. and John Francis Mercer, disapproved of the Constitution and were absent for its signing. Nine delegates, Oliver Ellsworth, Caleb Strong, William Pierce, William Houstoun, Alexander Martin, William Richardson Davie, William Churchill Houston, George Wythe and James McClurg, approved of the Constitution but were absent at the time of its signing. John Dickinson could not be present for the signing, but he arranged for a fellow delegate to sign his name. Edmund Randolph, George Mason and Elbridge Gerry were not absent, but they did not sign the Constitution. Six delegates, Nicholas Gilman, Jared Ingersoll, Richard Bassett, John Blair, William Few and William Blount, always voted for issues when they were there, but never said a word during the proceedings.

Listed below and on the next page are the names of the fifty-five delegates to the Constitutional Convention. Circle the names of those that signed the Constitution.

New Hampshire
John Langdon
Nicholas Gilman

Massachusetts
Elbridge Gerry
Nathaniel Gorham
Rufus King
Caleb Strong

New York
Robert Yates
Alexander Hamilton
John Lansing, Jr.

New Jersey
David Brearley
William Churchill Houston
William Paterson
William Livingston
Jonathan Dayton

Pennsylvania
Thomas Mifflin
Robert Morris
George Clymer
Jared Ingersoll
Thomas FitzSimons
James Wilson
Gouverneur Morris
Benjamin Franklin

Delaware
George Read
Gunning Bedford, Jr.
John Dickinson
Richard Bassett
Jacob Broom

Maryland
James McHenry
Daniel of St. Thomas Jenifer
Daniel Carroll
John Francis Mercer
Luther Martin

Virginia
George Washington
Edmund Randolph
John Blair
James Madison, Jr.
George Mason
George Wythe
James McClurg

South Carolina
John Rutledge
Charles Pinckney
Charles Cotesworth Pinckney
Pierce Butler

Georgia
William Few
Abraham Baldwin
William Pierce
William Houstoun

North Carolina
Alexander Martin
William Richardson Davie
Richard Dobbs Spaight
William Blount
Hugh Williamson

Connecticut
William Samuel Johnson
Roger Sherman
Oliver Ellsworth

How many delegates signed the Constitution? _____
There was actually one more person that signed it. His name was William Jackson. He was secretary of the Convention. How many actual signers were there? _____
In which states did all the delegates sign the Constitution? _____

_____

In which state did only one delegate sign? _____
How many delegates actually did not approve the Constitution? _____

Which states had the most delegates that did not approve it? _____

_____

Which state had the largest delegation? _____

Which had the smallest? _____ What did they have in common? _____

FATHERS OF OUR COUNTRY

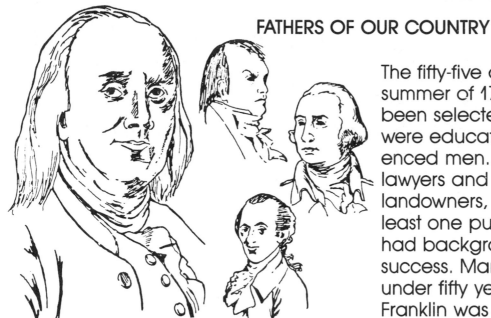

The fifty-five delegates who met in the summer of 1787 in Philadelphia had been selected by their states. They were educated, patriotic and experienced men. Over half of them were lawyers and judges, a fourth were landowners, all of them had held at least one public office, and all of them had backgrounds of some financial success. Many of the delegates were under fifty years of age. Benjamin Franklin was the oldest at 81. Though there were many differences between the delegates' ideas, they were a daring, courageous and creative group of men who were willing to take steps to establish a stronger national government. They debated, wrote and rewrote the Constitution during the summer of 1787. Although all the delegates were not always present, they had the opportunity for input into the document that is now the law of our land. Because the Constitution is the basis for our country and the product of their hard work, the men who wrote it have been named the Fathers of Our Country.

Write **True** or **False** to the following statements.

_____ Many of the delegates' backgrounds were similar.

_____ Only the men who were present all the time are the Fathers of Our Country.

_____ Many of the delegates were young.

_____ The delegates were young and inexperienced.

_____ The delegates disagreed on many of the ideas in the Constitution.

_____ No candidate was older than 81.

_____ The purpose of writing the Constitution was to make laws.

_____ Only special candidates were allowed to present ideas.

_____ Only one draft of the Constitution was made.

_____ Anyone who wanted to be a delegate could come to the Constitutional Convention.

_____ The Constitution presents the laws for running our country.

_____ Benjamin Franklin was too old to be a delegate.

_____ Less than fifty-five men wrote the Constitution.

_____ Writing the Constitution was not easy.

READING THE CONSTITUTION

Look at a copy of the entire Constitution. It is only 4,300 words long. After you have looked at it, answer the questions or fill in the blanks below.

The Constitution is divided into _____ main parts.

They are the _____, _____ and _____.

What is the purpose of the Preamble? _____

_____

_____

There are ___ Articles in the Constitution. Many of them have several sections. Tell which article provides for the following services or laws.

United States court system _____

The nation's debts and upholding the Constitution _____

The lawmaking body or the government _____

What must be done for the Constitution to be law _____

(That process was called _____.)

Explains the duties of the President _____

Allows for changes to be made in the Constitution _____

(That process is called _____.)

Tells what the states can do and what the federal government can do_____

There are ___ Amendments in the Constitution.

What makes the Constitution a usable document today? _____

_____

_____

Which Article has allowed it to be an up-to-date document? _____

Define the following words as they relate to the Constitution.

ARTICLE _____

AMENDMENT _____

_____

RATIFY _____

THREE BRANCHES OF GOVERNMENT

BRANCH

Headed by _____

_____ _____   _____   _____

_____

_____   _____   _____

_____   _____   _____

_____   _____   _____

_____   _____   _____

_____   _____   _____

                     _____   _____

The Founding Fathers did not want all the powers given to the government to be controlled by one man, or even just a few men. They feared if a small group was given too much power, the United States would once again be ruled by a tyrannical government like it had been under England. To avoid such a situation they divided the new government into three branches: the executive, the legislative and the judicial. The executive branch is headed by the President of the United States who carries out federal laws and recommends new ones, directs national defense and foreign policy and performs ceremonial duties. The legislative branch is headed by Congress which consists of the House of Representatives and the Senate. Their main task is to make the laws. The judicial branch is headed by the Supreme Court. This branch interprets the laws, decides cases in which federal laws apply and settles troubles between states. The Constitution built in a "check and balance" system so that no one branch could become too powerful. Each branch is controlled by the other two in several ways. The President may veto a law passed by Congress, but Congress may override his veto with a two-thirds vote. The Senate must approve any treaty the President makes and approve many of the appointments he makes. Any money the President needs for national defense must come from the Congress. The Supreme Court may check the Congress or the President by declaring a law unconstitutional. And, the Court is appointed by the other two and may be impeached by Congress.

Label the branches of the government above and write in their Constitutional duties.

CHECK AND BALANCE

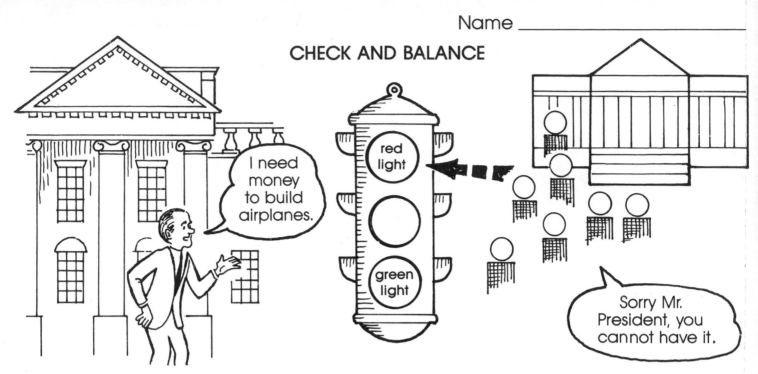

Fill in the chart below. Use the information from the preceding page.

POWER	HOW IT CAN BE CHECKED
Congress passes a law.	The President may
	The President may
	The Supreme Court may
The President vetoes a law passed by Congress.	Congress may
The President appoints a Supreme Court judge.	The Senate may
A Supreme Court judge shows misconduct in office.	Congress may
The President makes a treaty with another country.	The Senate may
President enforces a law.	The Supreme Court may
The President asks for money for defense.	Congress may

IF8750 U.S. Government

THE HOUSE OF REPRESENTATIVES

One of the two lawmaking bodies established as the result of the Great Compromise was the House of Representatives. It is often just called the House. The Constitution provided for its members, called representatives, to be elected by eligible voters in the states. The House is also called the Lower House because it has always been the lawmaking body elected by the people every two years. This name goes back to when the common man was represented in the Lower House in England. The House is the larger of the two lawmaking bodies of Congress.

The Constitution states the qualifications for a representative. Look in Article I, Section 2, paragraph 2 and tell what the qualifications are. _____

_____

_____

_____

The Constitution says the members of the House of Representatives should select a Speaker from its membership to preside over its meetings. All representatives have legal immunity as members of the House. That means they are protected for anything they write or say while in office. The Constitution also stated that all representatives be paid for their service.

The Constitution gave Congress the power to determine the size of the House and to divide the representation in each state according to population, and it also provided at least one representative per state. Originally there was a representative for every 30,000 people in a state. Now there is one for about every 500,000 citizens. Six states, Alaska, Delaware, North Dakota, South Dakota, Vermont and Wyoming, have one representative today. California has the most representatives with forty-five. A census is required every ten years by the Constitution so the number of representatives may be reapportioned if necessary. When the first House met, fifty-nine members were present. At the end of the first session there were sixty-five. In 1929 legislation was passed limiting the number of representatives allowed.

KNOWING ABOUT THE HOUSE

Use the previous page to help you fill in the blanks below. The circled letters in the answers will spell out the number of representatives the House is limited to now.

__ __ __ __Ⓞ__ __ __ __ __ has more representatives than any other state.

The number of representatives allotted per state is based on its

__Ⓞ__ __ __ __ __ __ __ __ __.

A __ __ __ __Ⓞ__ is taken every ten years to keep the population count up-to-date.

There is a representative for every __ __ __ __

__ __ __ __Ⓞ__ __ __ __Ⓞ__Ⓞ__ __Ⓞ__ citizens in a state.

One state alloted only one representative isⓄ__ __ __ __ __ __Ⓞ__.

The Lower House was so named inⓄ__ __ __ __ __ __Ⓞfirst because it represented the common man.

There were __ __ __Ⓞ__-__ __ __ __ representatives when the first House met.

Originally there was a representative for every __ __ __ __ __ __

__Ⓞ__ __ __ __ __ __ people in a state.

__ __ __ __Ⓞ__ __ is allotted only one

__ __ __Ⓞ__ __ __ __ __Ⓞ__ __ __ __ __.

When the first House session ended there were __ __ __ __Ⓞ-Ⓞ__ __ __ representatives present.

All representatives have legal __ __ __ __ __ __Ⓞ__ __.

A representative must be __ __ __ __ __ __ __-__ __ⓄⓄyears old to be elected to the House of Representatives.

The number of members in the House is limited to

__ __ __ __   __ __ __ __ __

__ __ __ __ __ __ __-__ __ __ __ __.

Name _____

THE SENATE

The other lawmaking body of Congress is the Senate. It is also called the Upper House. Both bodies have about the same amount of power. The Senate can introduce all types of legislation except spending bills. Only the Senate can approve or reject treaties and certain Presidential nominations for government offices.

Originally the Constitution gave each state legislature the power to select the senators from its state, but that was changed in 1913 by the 17th Amendment. Now voters in each state elect them. There is equal representation from each state in the Senate. Two senators are elected regardless of the states' population. A senator is elected every six years. No two senators are elected for six year terms at the same time from one state.

The Constitution states the qualifications for being a senator. Look at Article I, Section 3, paragraph 3 and tell what the qualifications are. _____

_____

_____

The only duty given the Vice President of the United States in the Constitution is that of president of the Senate. The Vice President presides over the sessions of the Senate but may only vote in case of a tie. The Senators choose a President pro tem from their membership to preside over the sessions when the Vice President cannot be there. The Constitution provides all senators legal immunity and compensation for their services.

Only twice have the qualifications of a senator been questioned. Follow the correct path to the Capitol to find out what they were.

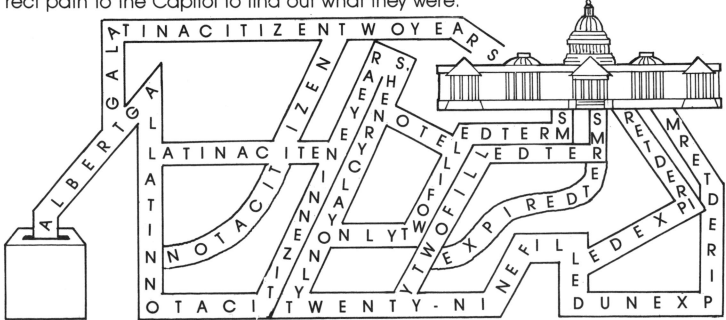

MAKING LAWS

LET ME INTRODUCE YOU.

BILL

Both senators and representatives may introduce bills, but only members of the House may introduce bills that deal with taxes or spending. Both houses of Congress must pass identical versions of a bill before it can become law. Once a bill is introduced in either house, it goes through almost the same process.

When a bill is (1) introduced it is assigned to a (2) committee for consideration. If a committee does not think a bill is worthy of further consideration, it (3A) tables it. If the committee thinks otherwise, it (3B) releases it for the entire house's consideration. Most bills are often passed in the House without any opposition. But if there is some disagreement, there can be a debate. The amount of time allowed for the debate is set by its rules committee. In the Senate the rules allow a senator to speak as long as he wants. A senator may choose to filibuster to block a vote, but the Senate may vote cloture to end a filibuster or limit a debate.

When a bill is (4) passed by either house it is (5) sent to the other for its input and consideration. Any differences between either lawmaking body is worked out by a (6) joint conference committee. When (7) both houses agree, the bill is signed by the Speaker and the Vice President. Then it is (8) sent to the President for his signature.

Answer the following questions.

Who may introduce a bill? _____

What is the only exception? _____

_____

What is the first thing that happens to a bill when it is introduced? _____

_____

If the committee does not like the bill it may table it. What does that mean? ____

_____

Define filibuster. _____

Define cloture. _____

Who sets the time limits for debates? _____

_____

Name _____

A LAW— IT'S UP TO ME.

BILL sign

BILL VETO

Once a bill has been approved by the House and the Senate, it is sent to the President. The President may do one of several things. (9A) He may sign it and send it back to the house in which it originated, and it will become law. (9B) If he does not approve the bill, he may veto it. That is, he may return it unsigned to the house in which it originated before listing his reasons for disapproval. (B1) Congress may make changes that will meet with the President's wishes, but if it wants the bill to remain as it is, (B2) two-thirds of both houses must vote for it as is and the bill will become law in spite of the President's veto. (9C) If the President does not act on a bill sent to him by Congress within ten working days after receiving it, the bill automatically becomes law. (9D) If Congress adjourns before the ten day period is up and the President has not signed the bill, the bill does not become law.

Use the information on this page and the previous one to show the different steps and routes a bill may take. Clue: Let the numbers help you.

1. _____

2. _____

3A. _____ 3B. _____

4. _____

5. _____

6. _____

7. _____

8. _____

9A. _____ 9B. _____ 9C. _____ 9D. _____

_____ _____ _____ _____

_____ _____ _____ _____

_____ _____ _____

B1. _____ B2. _____

_____ _____

IMPEACHMENT

House

Senate

The House of Representatives has the power to impeach all government officials except members of Congress. Each house may punish its own members for disorderly behavior. Impeachment is the charge of misconduct against an official in office. A majority vote is needed by House members to bring impeachment charges against a government official. The Senate has the power to try impeachment cases. A two-thirds vote is necessary for conviction. If an official is found guilty, the official may be removed from office and never allowed to hold a United States government position again. But a conviction does not mean prison or a fine. The case would have to be tried in a regular court for that type of punishment to occur. When a President is tried, the chief justice of the Supreme Court presides. The Vice President presides over all other impeachment cases. Why do you think the Vice President does not preside over an impeachment trial if the President is being tried?

The House of Representatives has brought impeachment charges only twelve times. There have been only four convictions. All four were judges. One President, the 17th, was impeached for several crimes while in office. He was found guilty by thirty-five senators and acquitted by nineteen—one short of the two-thirds necessary to convict an official.

Fill in the answers below and that President's name will appear in the boxes reading down.

1. Who presides over the trial of the President?
   _ _ _ _ _ ☐ _ _ _ _ _ _

2. Who brings impeachment charges?
   _ ☐ _ _ _

3. What vote is needed for conviction?
   _ _ _ - _ ☐ _ _ _ _

4. The House may not charge members of ___ .
   _ _ ☐ _ _ _ _ _ _

5. Who tries impeachment cases?
   ☐ _ _ _ _ _

6. How many convictions have there been?
   _ ☐ _ _

7. How many Presidents have been tried?
   _ ☐ _

COMPARING THE TWO HOUSES

Label the two houses under their pictures. Then fill in the rest of the blanks correctly.

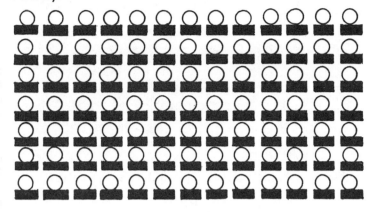   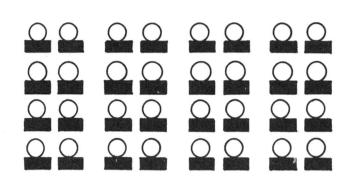

_____   _____

How can you tell?

_____

_____

What is another name for each house?

_____   _____

These two houses together are called _____ .

A member of this house is   A member of this house is

called a _____ .   called a _____ .

Write the qualifications for each house member.

Age: _____   Age: _____

Citizenship: _____   Citizenship: _____

Residence: _____   Residence: _____

_____   _____

Length of term: _____   Length of term: _____

Presiding Officer: _____   Presiding Officer: _____

                                             Alternate: _____

Impeachment Power: _____   Impeachment Power: _____

What vote is necessary to get   What vote is necessary to get convic-

impeachment? _____   tion? _____

Introduction of Bills: _____   Introduction of Bills: _____

_____   _____

Passage of Bill: _____   Passage of Bill: _____

_____   _____

Members of both houses receive a _____ for their services.

Members of both houses have _____ for anything
they say or write while in office.

Name _____

THE EXECUTIVE BRANCH

The President heads the executive branch of the United States. In what Article of the Constitution are the duties of the President stated?

_____

In Section 1, paragraph 1 of that Article it states the length of the President's term. What is it? _____ Who else is elected at the same time and for the same time period?

_____

What are the three qualifications a person must have to be President? _____

_____

Section 2 of the above Article states what the President's duties are. Place a check mark next to the duties given to the President by the Constitution.

____ The President may make treaties by himself.

____ The President appoints the Vice President.

____ The President is commander in chief of the armed forces.

____ The President makes appointments of ambassadors with the approval of the Senate.

____ The President sees that federal laws are carried out as they are designed.

____ The President does not tell Congress what he wants.

____ The President has the Congress greet visiting ambassadors.

____ The President may make treaties with the approval of the Senate.

____ The President commissions officers in the armed forces.

Write the oath a president must take before entering the Presidency—Article II, Section 1, paragraph 8.

_____

_____

_____

_____

_____

_____

Name _____

THE ELECTORAL COLLEGE

The Electoral College was created by the Constitution because the Founding Fathers did not want the President elected by Congress or the people. It is a group of delegates chosen by the voters to elect the President and Vice President. On Election Day, the first Tuesday after the first Monday in November, voters mark a ballot for President and Vice President. They do not actually vote for the candidates, but they select electors, or delegates, to represent their state in the Electoral College. Each state has as many votes in the Electoral College as it has Senators and Representatives. There are 538 electors. The electors meet in December on a date set by law to cast their votes. The results are sent to the president of the Senate who opens them. A candidate must receive 270 or a majority of the electoral votes to win. After two representatives from each body of Congress has counted the Electoral votes, the results are officially announced in January. The public knows the results right after the November election because the news media figured them out. They are not official until the Electoral votes have been counted by Congress. A candidate may win the popular vote but lose the election.

Answer **True** or **False** to the following statements. The circled letters in the **True** answers spell out the names of two Presidents who lost the popular vote but won the election.

_____ The electoral results are announced in January.

_____ The Founding Fathers did not want Congress to select the President.

_____ Each state has the same number of electors.

_____ The first Tuesday after the first Monday in November is Election Day.

_____ December is when the Electoral College meets.

_____ Voters actually vote for the delegates.

_____ Congress and the public nominate the candidates.

_____ A ballot is marked by voters in November.

_____ A majority of Electoral votes make a winner.

_____ There are five hundred thirty-eight electors.

_____ The election for President is the first Tuesday in December.

_____ It takes two hundred seventy votes to win the Presidency.

The two Presidents are _____.

THE JUDICIAL BRANCH

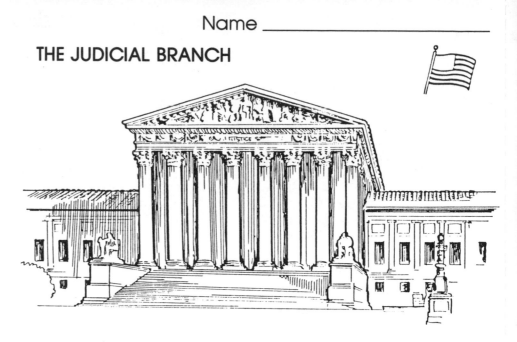

The Supreme Court heads the **judicial** branch of the United States government. It is the only court established by the **Constitution**. What Article in the Constitution states the limits of the Supreme Court? _____

The Supreme Court usually makes decisions of **national** importance. The Court acts within the laws stated in the Constitution. Because the wording of the Constitution is sometimes hard to understand, it can be difficult to interpret the law. That is one of the duties of the Supreme Court. When the Court does make a decision, all other courts in the country must follow that decision to guarantee equal legal justice to all Americans. The Constitution also gives the Supreme Court the power to judge whether **federal**, **state** and **local** governments are acting within the law and also to decide if an action of the President is constitutional.

Answer the questions below. The circled letters in the answers when unscrambled will spell out what a judge in the Supreme Court is called.

The Supreme Court usually only
hears what kind of cases?
__ __ ◯ __ __ __ __ __

What laws guide the Supreme Court's decisions?
__ __ __   __ __ __ ◯ __ __ ◯ __ __ __ __ __

The Supreme Court heads what
branch of the government?
◯ __ __ __ ◯ __ __

What other courts are there in the United States that must follow the decisions of the Supreme Court?
__ __ __ ◯ __ __ __ __, __ __ __ __ __ __, __ __ ◯ __ __

What is a judge that sits on the Supreme Court bench called?
__ __ __ __ __ __ __ __ __

POWERS OF THE FEDERAL GOVERNMENT

You must elect a state flower!

You cannot tell me how to run the state!

The federal government in the United States divides the powers between the national government and the states. In writing the Constitution the Founding Fathers knew they had to leave enough powers with the states or the Constitution would never be approved. All states were granted the rights to control all matters relating to that state that would not interfere with other states' governments or with the national interest.

Read Section 8 of Article I in the Constitution. List the eighteen powers Congress has in your own words. Number them.

_____
_____
_____
_____
_____
_____
_____
_____
_____
_____
_____
_____
_____
_____
_____
_____
_____
_____
_____
_____
_____
_____
_____
_____
_____
_____

THE RELATIONSHIP BETWEEN STATES AND THE FEDERAL GOVERNMENT

The Constitution states in Article IV the rights a citizen has in one state are the same in all the others. All states must honor the laws made in every other state, but Congress may make laws to say how those laws are carried out. This is how the Constitution attempted to keep the United States as one nation instead of separate states. This Article also states how new states may be made, and it guarantees every state its own form of government with federal help if called for by the governor.

Why do you think the rights should be the same in all states?

_____

_____

_____

Why should states honor each other's laws?

_____

_____

_____

Congress may bring a new state into the nation, but a new state may not be made by dividing an already existing one into two states, nor can two states combine to make one state. Do you think this is a good idea? _____ Explain your answer.

_____

_____

_____

Why would every state want to have its own government?

_____

_____

_____

When might a governor call on the federal government for help?

_____

_____

_____

Name _____

AMENDING THE CONSTITUTION

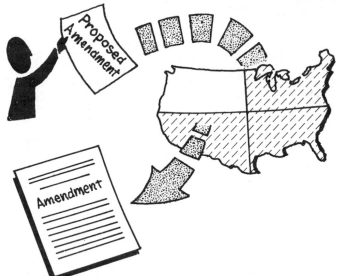

The Constitution has been a lasting document. Written over 200 years ago, its authors realized times would change so they provided a way the Constitution could be changed when necessary. Which Article provides for such changes? _____

What is a change in the Constitution called?

_____

A change to the Constitution may be proposed when either two-thirds of Congress or two-thirds of the states request it. To be accepted as part of the Constitution, the proposed amendment must be ratified by three-fourths of the states. It is not easy to make Constitutional changes. Over 9,000 amendments have been proposed over the years, but only 26 have been ratified by three-fourths of the states. Even with popular support from the population at large, such as the Equal Rights Amendment recently had, ratification is not always assured. Currently three suggestions are being considered for Constitutional reform:

1) Change treaty ratification from two-thirds approval by the Senate to sixty percent.
2) Congress should authorize a limit to campaign spending.
   Terms for members of the House of Representatives should be four years rather than two.

Citizens-at-large can have input into making changes by writing to their congressmen. Select one of the above. Circle the one you chose. Write a letter to a congressman telling him how you feel about the suggestion under consideration and how you would like him to vote. Back up your feelings with good reasons.

_____

_____

_____

_____

_____

_____

_____

_____

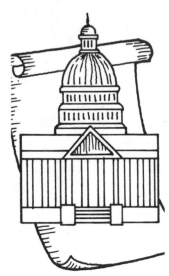

A FEDERAL GOVERNMENT

The Constitution designed a federal government—a system which divided the powers of the national government and those of the states. In some areas the national government was in control in such things as war, treaties, trade, land matters, money and post offices. Each state controlled what went on within it, and that did not affect the nation.

Write **N** in front of the powers below if they are controlled by the national government. Write **S** if they are controlled by the states.

___ A tax is placed on products coming to America from foreign countries.

___ Money is given to repair state roads.

___ An agreement is reached between a European country and America.

___ A new stamp is designed to commemorate the signing of the Constitution.

___ Speed limits on rural highways are established.

___ A child must be of a certain age before entering public school.

___ The borders between two states will be a river.

___ The election day date for state officials was set.

___ Money was alloted to build five new aircraft carriers for the United States Navy.

___ Children must attend school until they reach a certain age.

___ The value of money is established.

___ Anyone making fake money or stamps will be punished.

___ A limit was passed on the number of new immigrants allowed to come to America each year.

___ Every driver of an automobile must have a license.

___ There are rules for becoming an American citizen.

___ A citizen will be fined for going through a stop sign.

___ A government official will be tried for selling information to a foreign government.

ODDS AND ENDS

Supreme Law

State Law

Local Law

Article VI makes a few final statements about the national debt, the order of the laws in the United States, and that every official at all levels must support the Constitution.

The authors of the Constitution promised that all outstanding debts would be paid back in the first paragraph of this Article. In the second paragraph they said that federal laws were the "supreme law". That is, the Constitution, laws made by Congress, and treaties of the government were above state and local laws. The final paragraph says that officials at every level must support the Constitution of the United States first and that they never will have to take a religious test to be a government official.

The order of laws in the United States is listed below. Fill in the name of the place (city, state, town) from which they are administered. The first one will be the same for everyone. The next two will be a matter of where you live.

1. "Supreme Law" _____

2. State Laws _____ (state and capital)

3. Local Laws _____ (city or town)

Answer **TRUE** or **FALSE** to the following statements.

_____ Every state legislator must support the United States Constitution before supporting his or her state constitution.

_____ The United States owed money before the Constitution was written.

_____ The Constitution's Article VI is its most important one.

_____ The Constitution, laws made by Congress, and treaties are the highest laws in the land.

_____ Judges in every state and city must obey the laws of the Constitution.

_____ It is necessary to take a religious test before becoming a government official.

_____ Article VI wraps up some details after the Constitution defined the powers of the federal and state governments.

RATIFYING THE CONSTITUTION

Because the writers of the Constitution had not been given the authority by their states to write the document, it had to be sent to each state for approval. Before it could be sent to the states, it had to be written in good, easy-to-read form. The delegates asked Gouverneur Morris, an excellent writer, to write it. He did and in two days he completed its 4,300 words. On September 17, 1787, thirty-nine of the fifty-five delegates signed it and sent it to the states for ratification. Which Article in the Constitution provided the rules for its ratification? _____ Special conventions were held in each state to approve it. How many states needed to approve the Constitution before it could become law? ____.

People against the Constitution were afraid individual rights were not guaranteed. George Mason, Elbridge Gerry and Patrick Henry spoke out against it. Alexander Hamilton, James Madison and John Jay wrote eighty-five letters supporting its passage. They claimed the check and balance system would create a strong central government and yet preserve states' rights.

Take one side or the other and fight for or against ratification of the Constitution.

_____

_____

_____

_____

_____

_____

_____

_____

_____

_____

_____

_____

THE BILL OF RIGHTS

The delegates of the Constitutional Convention had seen no need for a bill of rights because of the limitations set on the federal government by the constitution, and because most of the states had their own bill of rights. But the citizenry felt differently. When the Constitution was sent to the states for ratification, some people would not approve it until there was a bill of rights specifically listing the individual rights of every citizen. Others ratified it with the promise there would be a bill of rights. When the first Congress met in 1789, it immediately took several amendments that had been suggested during the ratification process under consideration. James Madison wrote twelve of them which were again presented to the states for ratification. Ten were approved. They make up the Bill of Rights or the First Ten Amendments to the Constitution. Because they were written and adopted so soon after the original Constitution, they are considered a part of it.

The first amendment lists five freedoms. Circle them.

RELIGION	BREAKING THE LAW	SPEECH	HURTING OTHERS
PRESS	GATHERING PEACEFULLY IN A GROUP	TREASON	PETITION

Which Amendment states a search warrant is necessary before any citizen's possessions may be looked at and seized? _____

Amendments 5 and 6 deal with citizens' rights in courts. Check the ones below that are true.

___ No person may be tried twice for the same crime if found not guilty.

___ Anyone can be tried for a serious crime without a grand jury's indictment (a formal charge).

___ No person must speak against himself.

___ A person may be tried without a jury.

___ Witnesses can be a part of a person's trial.

___ Life, liberty and property can not be taken without due process of law.

Name _____

MORE ABOUT THE BILL OF RIGHTS

Which other Amendment deals with jury trials? _____

Which Amendment provides an army for defense and the right for people to own guns for their protection? _____

Soldiers can live in private homes in time of war if prescribed by Congress. Otherwise they may only do so with permission of the owner. Which Amendment states this? _____

Read Amendment 8. What is bail? _____

_____

What three things does Amendment 8 forbid? _____

_____

The authors of the Bill of Rights could not list every individual right, so they put in the 9th and 10th Amendments to cover those not listed. What might some rights be that were not specifically listed? _____

_____

Look at the pictures. Tell which amendment protects the pictured right. If it is not a specific right listed write 9 and 10.

AMENDMENTS

Nothing is perfect—and certainly not forever. The Founding Fathers realized this when they provided for changes in the Constitution. Amendments to the Constitution have either been additions to or changes of the original document. Since the Bill of Rights was added to the Constitution in 1791, only sixteen amendments have been ratified.

    Listed below on the left are the Amendments and the dates they became part of the Constitution. On the right are what the Amendments are about in a scrambled order. Read a copy of the Amendment section of the Constitution and write the Amendment's number on the line in front of its definition.

Amendment 11 (1795)
Amendment 12 (1804)
Amendment 13 (1865)
Amendment 14 (1868)
Amendment 15 (1870)
Amendment 16 (1913)
Amendment 17 (1913)
Amendment 18 (1919)
Amendment 19 (1920)
Amendment 20 (1933)
Amendment 21 (1933)
Amendment 22 (1951)
Amendment 23 (1961)
Amendment 24 (1964)
Amendment 25 (1967)
Amendment 26 (1971)

____ Repealed 18th Amendment but allowed states that wanted, to keep it.

____ Described rights of citizens, representation and voting, and defined the obligation of oath takers and Civil War debts.

____ Says no one may be kept from voting because of non-payment of a tax.

____ Did away with slavery.

____ Gave vote to citizens eighteen and older.

____ Gave women the right to vote.

____ Limited length of presidential term.

____ Changes who elects senators.

____ Provided for succession to the presidency and presidential disability.

____ Gave everyone the right to vote.

____ Changed the dates of the President and Vice President's term in office

____ Would not allow liquor to be made or sold.

____ Gave people who live in Washington, D.C. the right to vote in presidential elections.

____ Explained what kind of cases federal courts could try.

____ Established the income tax.

____ Changed how the Electoral College voted.

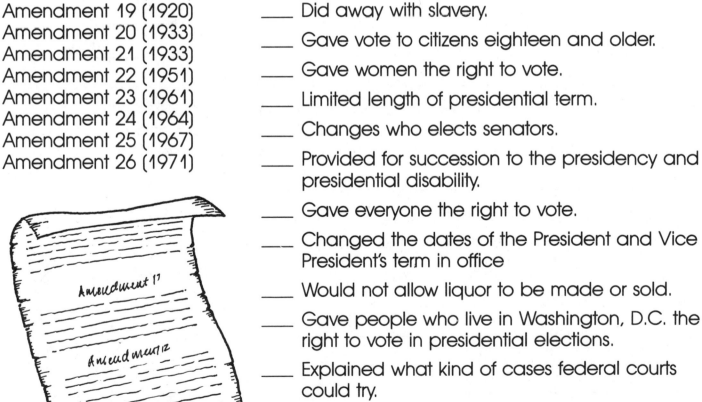

Amendment 17

Amendment 12

AMENDMENT 11

Amendment 11 changes one part of Article III, Section 2 in the Constitution. Article III, Section 2 tells what cases will be heard by a federal court. Amendment 11 says that if a person from one state or a foreign country thinks he or she has something against another state, he or she can not get the case heard in any federal court.

Why do you think this Amendment was written? _____
_____
_____

What might be a circumstance where a state did something to a citizen of another state, that the citizen thought unfair? _____
_____
_____

If a citizen of one state thought he or she had something against another state, at what level could he or she be heard? _____
_____

Suppose you and your family were touring in a neighboring state's capitol building and the ceiling caved in on all of you. Your father received a concussion from the falling cement and the rest of you received bad cuts and bruises. What would you do? _____
_____

Explain how you would go about it and what you would claim?
_____
_____
_____
_____
_____
_____
_____

AMENDMENTS 12, 20, 22 AND 25

Amendments 12, 20, 22 and 25 have something to do with the executive branch.

Amendment 12 changed Article II Section 1, paragraph 3. It was written after Thomas Jefferson and Aaron Burr tied for President, and the House of Representatives had to select a President. The electors used to vote for two candidates. They did not specify which one was for President. The one with the most votes became President and the runner-up became Vice President. Amendment 12 changed that procedure. The electors had to vote for one man for President and another for Vice President. Another change Amendment 12 made was that if no person received a majority of the electoral votes, the House of Representatives would have to elect a President from the three highest on the list. The Constitution had said it should choose from the five highest on the list.

The House of Representatives had to elect a President one other time, in 1825. Answer **True** or **False** to the following statements to find out who it was. The circled letters in the True answers will spell out that President's name.

_____ Amen(d)ment 12 changed the d(a)te the electors met to elec(t) a President.

_____ The (J)efferson-Burr tie caused Amendment 12 t(o) be written.

_____ The (H)ouse of Represe(n)tatives is re(qu)ired to elect a Pres(i)dent when there is not a majority for one ca(n)didate.

_____ Aaron Bur(r) and Thomas (J)efferson shar(e)d the preside(n)cy.

_____ Arti(c)le I deals wit(h) the executive br(a)nch.

_____ Originally ele(c)tors did not have to specif(y) which candid(a)te they wanted as Presi(d)ent.

_____ (A)mend(m)ent(s) 12, 20, 22 and 25 deal with the presidency.

The name of the other President elected by the House of Representatives was

___ ___ ___ ___ ___   ___ ___ ___ ___ ___ ___   ___ ___ ___ ___ ___ .

Amendment 12 referred to the fourth day of March being the starting date of the presidential term. Amendment 20, adopted almost 130 years later, changed the term of the President and Vice President to begin at noon on the twentieth day of January. This was done so there would not be such a long period of time between the election in November and when the President took office. Originally that much time was needed because transportation was not good and it took time for a newly elected President to reach the capital. Now a President can be in Washington in a matter of hours. An outgoing President is considered a "lame duck". Before the date change, the country was at a standstill the four months between the election and inauguration dates. This section is the most important part of Amendment 20.

Amendment 20 makes other changes and additions to the Constitution. The second part changes Article I, Section 4, paragraph 2 of the Constitution. It says Congress must meet at least once a year and that meeting is to begin at noon on January third. In the beginning Congress only met once a year or when the President called a special session. Now they meet almost year round. The rest of Amendment 20 explains how a President will be chosen if a President-elect dies before taking office and the procedures necessary to get Amendment 20 approved.

Amendment 20 is often called the Lame Duck Amendment. Why do you think it is called that? _____

_____

What is a "lame duck" President? _____

_____

Why was there such a long period between election day and inauguration day? __

_____

Why is it different now? _____

_____

What other change did Amendment 20 make to the Constitution? _____

_____

When did Congress meet before? _____

What addition did it make to the Constitution?_____

_____

Continuation of Amendments 12, 20, 22 and 25

Amendment 22 was written after Franklin D. Roosevelt was elected to his fourth term. There had been no limit in the Constitution to the number of terms a President could serve. Until Roosevelt's time, no President had served more than two terms. Many felt this was too long a time for one person to serve and so the twenty-second Amendment was written. Amendment 22 states that no person may be elected more than twice, and that anyone who has been President for more than two years of someone else's term cannot be elected more than once.

Amendment 25 changes and expands Article II, Section 1. It came about when Lyndon Johnson moved into the Presidency after John Kennedy was assassinated and there was no Vice President for almost fourteen months. Amendment 25 says when there is no Vice President the President should nominate one, and if half the Senate and House of Representatives vote in favor of the nomination, that person will be the Vice President. Death had been the only way a President had vacated the office until 1974. In 1974 President Nixon resigned. Gerald Ford, who had been appointed Vice President when the vice presidency was vacated earlier, took over the office of President. With the vice presidency again vacated, President Ford nominated Nelson Rockefeller for Vice President. The amendment worked. Amendment 25 also provides for the Vice President to take over the President's duties when the President is unable to perform his job. This part of the amendment proved it worked too. When President Reagan had surgery in 1985, Vice President Bush assumed the presidency for eight hours.

Why was Amendment 22 written? _____

_____

What is the most number of years a President could serve? _____

If a President can only be elected to two terms, then explain how he could serve

that number of years. _____

_____

_____

Continuation of Amendments 12, 20, 22 and 25

Tell under what circumstances the following were President.

Gerald Ford _____

George Bush _____

Franklin Roosevelt _____

Lyndon Johnson _____

Richard Nixon _____

Review of the Presidential Amendments

Give a title to each of the Presidential Amendments

Amendment 12 _____

Amendment 20 _____

Amendment 22 _____

Amendment 25 _____

Which amendment was written after there was a tie for the presidency? _____

Which one was partially written to see that the government was always run by an able person? _____

Which amendment was written to limit a President's length of service? _____

Which one redesigned how the President and Vice President were elected? _____

Which amendment changed the date the President took office? _____

Answer **True** or **False** to the following statements.

_____ A presidency is only vacated upon the President's death.

_____ Electors must specify one candidate for President and another for Vice President.

_____ A lame duck President is disabled.

_____ No President has ever held the office longer than ten years.

_____ One President acted as President for only eight hours.

_____ If the electors fail to give one candidate a majority of the votes for President, the Senate elects a President from one of the three highest vote getters.

_____ When Lyndon Johnson left the vice presidency to become President, there was no Vice President.

_____ Gerald Ford was not elected President.

_____ A person who has been President for more than two years of someone else's term cannot be elected more than once.

AMENDMENTS 13, 14 AND 15

Amendments 13, 14 and 15 are often called the Civil Rights Amendments. The Founding Fathers had so many disagreements about the treatment of slaves, that there almost was no Constitution. Slavery by name was not mentioned in the Constitution. Not until after the Civil War was slavery abolished. Amendment 13 gave black people their freedom.

The first section of Amendment 14 made black people citizens and entitled to the same rights guaranteed all citizens by the Constitution. Section 2 of this amendment changed Article 1, Section 2 of the Constitution. Every black is now counted as one person instead of three-fifths of a person. This section also imposes a penalty on any state that refuses to let all male citizens, twenty-one or over, vote. The rest of Amendment 14 controlled the positions federal officers who had joined the Confederacy might have and payment of the Union's Civil War debt.

Amendment 14 does give all adult males that are citizens the right to vote. Amendment 15 carries it a step further and states that no citizen may be kept from voting because of race, color or previous condition of servitude (slavery).

Solve the crossword.

Across

1. What was fought between the states?
3. Word not mentioned in the Constitution.
4. What Amendment 13 gave all black people.
6. The amendment that made blacks citizens.

Down

1. What Amendments 13, 14 and 15 are often called.
2. No citizen can be kept from voting because of this.
5. Every black is now counted as ____ person.

AMENDMENT 16

Amendment 16 gives Congress the right to tax individuals according to the amount of money they earn. It was first proposed as an amendment in 1894, but it was ruled unconstitutional by the Supreme Court. It became part of the Constitution in 1913. Until then the only way Congress got money to pay debts and provide the necessary defense for the country was through taxing imported items, and on items made, sold and used in the United States. Such taxes were the same in all the states. The income tax created by Amendment 16 raised much more money. When the amendment became law, a part of every person's salary was taken out for taxes. It was thought to be a fair tax because it was a way to give the government money for running the country according to each individual's ability to pay. More people probably complain more about Amendment 16 than any other amendment.

Do you think Amendment 16, the Income Tax Amendment, is a fair one? _____
Explain your answer. _____

_____

_____

_____

Think of some ways the government spends the money received from individuals' incomes. _____

_____

Why do you think people complain about Amendment 16? _____

_____

Take a poll. Ask several working people if they think paying an income tax is necessary, if it is fair, and if they can suggest other ways for the government to raise money.

#	NECESSARY?	FAIR?	OTHER WAYS
1			
2			
3			
4			

(Use back of page if necessary.)

Name _____

AMENDMENTS 18 AND 21

Amendment 18 is called the Prohibition Amendment. This amendment made it illegal to make, sell or ship any alcoholic beverages anywhere in the United States. It also prohibited exporting them out of or importing them into the country. Businesses that made or sold liquor had one year from the time Amendment 18 was passed to stop making it. A time limit of seven years for ratification was placed on this amendment. Since then, most amendments have given a seven year time limit from the time of proposal to ratification. One year after this amendment was ratified it became law. Fourteen years later Amendment 18 was repealed by Amendment 21. Amendment 21 withdrew the federal limitations on the manufacturing and selling of alcoholic beverages, but recognized the rights of individual states to still practice prohibition.

Define prohibition. _____

Define repeal. _____

Do you think a seven year limit for ratification is a good idea?_____Why or why not?

_____

_____

Why did it take one year after ratification for Amendment 18 to become effective?

_____

_____

Did Amendment 21 make prohibition illegal? _____ Explain your answer. _____

_____

Do you think laws should be made because they are best for the country or

because they are strong personal beliefs and morals? _____

Explain your answer. _____

_____

_____

_____

AMENDMENTS 17, 19, 23, 24 AND 26

VOTES FOR WOMEN

Amendments 17, 19, 23, 24 and 26 all have something to do with voting. They either changed parts or expanded the Constitution. Amendment 17 changed Article I, Section 3 of the Constitution. Amendment 17 gives the people the right to elect their senators. The 17th Amendment also directed the governor of a state to choose a vacated senatorial seat until the election could be held.

How were senators elected before Amendment 17? _____
_____ because the authors of the Constitution thought the general public would not be well enough informed to make the right choice.

How were vacancies filled before Amendment 17? _____
_____

Amendment 19 gave women the right to vote. This cancelled a part of Amendment 14. Explain how it did that. _____
_____

People living in the District of Columbia, the United States Capital, could not vote in Presidential elections because it was not a state. Amendment 23 gave them that right. Now the Capital has one elector that meets with the electors from all the states to elect the President and Vice President.

Why didn't the people in the country's capital vote for President before Amendment 23 became effective? _____

Amendment 24 ruled that no United States citizens could be kept from voting in a federal election because they had failed to pay taxes. Some states tried to keep some people from voting if they had not paid their taxes. Why do you think some states tried this? _____

Amendment 26 changed the age at which people could vote to 18. Although the Constitution said the age at which people could vote should be set by the states, one amendment stated the age. Which amendment was it and what age did it state? _____

Name _____

KNOW YOUR CONSTITUTION!

Circle the correct answer to each of the following questions.

How many delegates signed the Constitution?   50   40   39   44   55

Which amendments are sometimes referred to as the Civil Rights Amendments?
   11, 12, 13   12, 13, 14   13, 14, 15   14, 15, 16

What had to be done to ratify the Constitution?
   A Bill of Rights had to be written.
   The delegates had to sign it.
   Eighty-five letters written to support it.
   Nine states had to approve it.

Who was not a delegate, but signed the Constitution?
   William Jackson   Benjamin Franklin   George Mason
   Edmund Randolph   Gouverneur Morris

Which state did not attend the Constitutional Convention?
   Delaware   Georgia   New Hampshire   Rhode Island

Who was considered "Father of the Constitution?"
   George Washington   James Madison   Benjamin Franklin
   Roger Sherman   Alexander Hamilton

Which part of the Constitution has seven parts?
   Bill of Rights   Amendments   Articles   Preamble

Who may introduce all kinds of bills?
   The Supreme Court   The House of Representatives   The Senate
   Lobbyists   Citizens   The President

Who can veto a bill?
   A senator   A justice   The President   A representative

What document did the Constitution replace?
   Declaration of Independence   Articles of Confederation
   Bill of Rights   Federalist Papers

Which compromise is referred to as the Great Compromise?
   Two house legislature   Establishment of the Electoral College
   Slave 3/5 a person   Establishment of three branches
   Congress controlled interstate commerce and foreign trade.

Who is president of the Senate?
   The majority leader   The Chief Justice   The President
   The president pro tem   The Vice President

Who hears impeachment charges against a government official?
   The Senate   The Supreme Court   The Executive Branch
   The House of Representatives

MATCHING CONSTITUTIONAL FACTS

Write the letter in front of the fact or event on the left on the line to the right that goes with it.

A. This state refused to stop trading with England.
B. The Declaration of Independence
C. Five states came to the meeting.
D. Women given right to vote
E. City where Constitutional Convention held
F. It was abolished with Amendment 13.
G. Every state is given two.
H. Enforces the law
I. Check and balance system
J. The Virginia Plan
K. Needs to be thirty years old and a citizen for 9 years
L. Introduces all bills having to do with money
M. Signed the Declaration of Independence, the Articles of Confederation and the Constitution
N. The people do not like it.
O. Events were kept secret.
P. Describes the Legislature
Q. Have made the Constitution a lasting document
R. There are 9 of them.
S. Interprets the law
T. It elects the President and Vice President.
U. Assigned to a committee for consideration
V. Became Presidents of the United States
W. One of first things the first Congress did

___ A senator to be elected
___ George Washington and James Madison
___ Executive Branch
___ The Income Tax Amendment
___ Adoption July 4, 1776
___ House of Representatives
___ Article I
___ Annapolis Convention
___ Called for representation according to population
___ Amendments
___ Georgia
___ Senators
___ Robert Morris and Roger Sherman
___ Slavery
___ A bill that has been introduced
___ Supreme Court justices
___ Amendment 19
___ Judicial Branch
___ Three branches in the government
___ Philadelphia
___ Wrote the Bill of Rights
___ Electoral College
___ Constitutional Convention

MATCH THE ACTS WITH THE MAN!

The names of the men listed in alphabetical order on the left were all participants in the Constitutional Convention. The numbers after their names tell on what page some information may be found about them. Use these and the documents themselves to write the letter next to each fact on the line in front of each man's name if it describes that man. Some men will have more than one fact true about them.

_____ George Clymer

_____ Jonathan Dayton

_____ John Dickinson

_____ Benjamin Franklin 11

_____ Elbridge Gerry 34

_____ Alexander Hamilton 34

_____ William Jackson

_____ James Madison 10, 34

_____ George Mason 34

_____ Gouverneur Morris 34

_____ Robert Morris

_____ William Paterson 7

_____ George Read

_____ Edmund Rudolph

_____ Roger Sherman

_____ George Washington 6

_____ James Wilson

A. Secretary of the Convention

B. Actually wrote the words of the Constitution

C. Signed the Declaration of Independence

D. Youngest delegate at the Convention; was last in New Jersey delegation to sign the Constitution

E. President of the Convention

F. Oldest delegate at the Convention

G. A delegate from Connecticut and Robert Morris signed the Constitution, Declaration of Independence and the Articles of Confederation

H. Had another delegate from Delaware sign for him

I. Kept secret records of every session

J. Became President of the U.S.

K. Presented the New Jersey Plan

L. Authored several letters supporting ratification of Constitution

M. Suggested there be two law making bodies in Congress

N. Presented the Virginia Plan

O. "Father of the Constitution"

P. Spoke out against ratification of Constitution because it did not guarantee individual rights

Q. Signed Constitution twice—once under his name; once under the name of another delegate

R. Virginia's Governor; did not sign Constitution

CONSTITUTIONAL VOCABULARY

Write the definitions for the following words as they relate to the Constitution of the United States.

ABOLISH _____

AMENDMENT _____

BALLOT _____

BILL _____

CENSUS _____

CHIEF JUSTICE _____

CIVIL RIGHTS _____

COMPROMISE _____

DELEGATE _____

DUE PROCESS _____

ELECTOR _____

FEDERAL _____

IMPEACH _____

LAME DUCK _____

LEGISLATURE _____

MAJORITY _____

PETITION _____

PREAMBLE _____

PRESIDENT PRO TEM _____

QUORUM _____

RATIFY _____

REAPPORTION _____

SEIZURE _____

TREASON _____

VETO _____

Answer Key

George Washington

1st President

George Washington was a fourth generation American. He was raised on the family plantation. He had only seven or eight years of education. He was very good in math and became a surveyor by the age of fifteen. He was a leader in the French and Indian War, a gentleman farmer and a state legislator. He became angry about regulations Britain was enforcing and spoke out against them. He participated in the first Continental Congress and was elected Commander in Chief of the second. He led American troops for seven years before the British surrendered. Five years after the war, he was president of the Constitutional Convention. Once the Constitution was approved, he was elected president. Words spoken at his funeral sum up how the nation felt about him: "First in war, first in peace, and first in the hearts of his countrymen."

Born: February 22, 1732
Birthplace: Pope's Creek, Westmoreland County, Virginia
Political Party: Federalist
State Represented: Virginia
Term: April 30, 1789–March 3, 1797
Died: December 14, 1799
Vice President: John Adams (F)

DISCOVER FOR YOURSELF

Fill in the answer to each clue on the lines to the right.

Brother who cared for Washington after father died **Lawrence**
1 2 3 4 5 6 7 8

Where Washington was inaugurated **New York**
9 10 11 12 13 14 15

From whom Washington wanted to gain independence **British**
16 17 18 19 20 21 22

Where capitol moved during Washington's terms **Philadelphia**
23 24 25 26 27 28 29 30 31 32 33 34

Body that nominated him for president **Congress**
35 36 37 38 39 40 41 42

Fill in the letters whose number matches those under the lines below to learn what General spoke at Washington's funeral.

Henry "Light Horse" Lee
22 5 37 17 12   26 18 38 24 19   32 13 4 21 29   1 10 40

. . . AND AT THE SAME TIME
What did Eli Whitney develop during Washington's presidency? **cotton gin**

Page 1

John Adams

2nd President

John Adams was the eldest son of a farmer, John Adams, and Susanna Boylston, of a leading Massachusetts family. He was a Harvard graduate. He taught school briefly before practicing law. Adams was a leader against British colonial policies. He relished every act of opposition toward the British, and yet his high principles led him to defend British soldiers for their part in the Boston Massacre. As a delegate to the Continental Congress he was an advocate of independence. He was on the committee that wrote the Declaration of Independence. His most successful act as a diplomat was having The Netherlands recognize American sovereignty. He felt the vice presidency an "insignificant office". He was president during a controversial time, but kept the country out of war. Adams could be blunt, impatient and vain, but he had strong convictions which in time have been proven right.

Born: October 30, 1735
Birthplace: Braintree, (later Quincy), Massachusetts
Political Party: Federalist
State Represented: Massachusetts
Term: March 4, 1797–March 3, 1801
Died: July 4, 1826
Vice President: Thomas Jefferson Democratic-Republican

DISCOVER FOR YOURSELF

Circle the hidden words in the puzzle that answer the clues below. Answers appear forward, backward, down or diagonally. Write the answer to each clue on the line next to or under it.

Wife's first name **Abigail**

Two men that negotiated Treaty of Paris with him **Franklin, Jay**

Adams' age at death **ninety**

A British law passed in 1765 that levied higher taxes **Stamp Act**

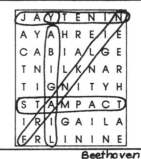

```
J A Y T E N I N
A Y A H R E I E
C A B I A L G E
T N I L K N A R
T I G N I T Y H
S T A M P A C T
I R I G A I L A
F R L I N I N E
```

. . . AND AT THE SAME TIME
A German composer that lived during Adams' time and was going deaf. **Beethoven**

Page 2

Thomas Jefferson

3rd President

THE LOUISIANA PURCHASE

Thomas Jefferson came from a family that valued education. Much of his early learning was with private tutors. He became head of the family at fourteen when his father died. After two years of college he studied law. Not only was he talented as a lawyer, but he was also skilled as an architect, inventor, farmer and musician. He was the main author of the Declaration of Independence. He felt strongly about the fight for freedom, but he had no desire to be a soldier. He felt more useful as a lawmaker. He was responsible for land reforms and the Bill of Rights. He fought for the common man and was a proponent of states' rights. His principles conflicted with the federalists. He formed the Democratic-Republican Party. The Louisiana Purchase and Lewis and Clark's Expedition were his biggest accomplishments as president—and important and lasting today.

Born: April 13, 1743
Birthplace: Shadwell, Virginia
Political Party: Democratic-Republican
State Represented: Virginia
Term: March 4, 1801–March 3, 1809
Died: July 4, 1826
Vice President: Aaron Burr (DR) George Clinton (DR)

DISCOVER FOR YOURSELF

Write the answer to each clue in the row of boxes to the right. Rearrange the circled letters on the lines below to name one of Jefferson's inventions.

His favorite hostess **DOLLEY MADISON**

He was minister to this country **FRANCE**

Where Lewis and Clark explored **NORTHWEST**

Name of his estate **MONTICELLO**

His vice president tried for treason **AARON BURR**

What Jefferson invented **dumb waiter**

. . . AND AT THE SAME TIME
What was the name of the steamboat that made the first successful trip between New York City and Albany, and who was on it? **Clermont; Robt. Fulton**

Page 3

James Madison

4th President

James Madison was a sickly child, the oldest of twelve. He received his early education from his parents, tutors and a private school. After he graduated from the College of New Jersey (now Princeton), he studied for the ministry but soon turned to politics. He served in Virginia's legislature, the Continental Congress, the Constitutional Convention, the senate and in Jefferson's administration as secretary of state before becoming president. Madison tried to stay out of war, but finally declared it June 18, 1812. After three years the war ended with no "winner". Madison was able to spend time directing the government in the national interest. The title, "Father of the Constitution" certainly belongs to Madison. Not only was he the primary author, but he defended and practiced it throughout his political career.

Born: March 16, 1751
Birthplace: Port Conway, Virginia
Political Party: Democratic-Republican
State Represented: Virginia
Term: March 4, 1809–March 3, 1817
Died: June 28, 1836
Vice President: George Clinton (DR) Elbridge Gerry (DR)

DISCOVER FOR YOURSELF

Write the answers to each clue or question in the row of boxes following. The number in the boxes where the letter E falls will add up to the number of states in the Union at the end of Madison's presidency.

The name of Madison's home **M O$_5$ N T$_8$ P$_2$ E$_2$ L I$_4$ E$_4$ R**

A book on political theory written by Madison and Alexander Hamilton and John Jay **T$_2$ H$_3$ E$_1$ F$_6$ E$_1$ D$_5$ E$_2$ R$_1$ A$_3$ L I$_7$ S$_8$ T$_3$**

After the battle against what fort was the Star-Spangled Banner written? **M$_2$ C$_3$ H$_6$ E$_1$ N$_7$ R$_2$ Y$_4$**

Madison was called this nickname by his friends **J$_4$ E$_2$ M M Y$_6$**

Number of states in the Union **19**

. . . AND AT THE SAME TIME
How are J.J. Audubon, Charles Wilson Peale and Jonathan Trumbull alike? **American Artists**

Page 4

James Monroe

5th President

Name _____

James Monroe was the son of a planter. After a tutorial and private school education he went to the College of William and Mary. He left there only a few months to join the army and fight in the Revolutionary War. After service he studied law with Jefferson who became his lifelong friend and advisor. As a politician he served in several state and national offices and in the administrations of Washington, Jefferson and Madison. Monroe was an aggressive statesman. He spoke his views. He was the main person responsible for negotiating the Louisiana Purchase. Monroe was popular as president. He was especially strong in foreign affairs. During his administration the United States obtained Florida, settled on the Canadian border and Oregon's occupation. His greatest accomplishment "The Monroe Doctrine" is the basis of our foreign policy today.

Born: April 28, 1758
Birthplace: Westmoreland County, Virginia
Political Party: Democratic-Republican
State Represented: Virginia
Term: March 4, 1817–March 3, 1825
Died: July 4, 1831
Vice President: Daniel Tompkins (DR)

DISCOVER FOR YOURSELF

Write the answer to each clue in the row of boxes to the right.

What is the surprise vertical word? **Monroe**

President for whom Monroe was Secretary of State?
1. MADISON

Person with a strong love for his country?
2. PATRIOT

Settlers in America
3. COLONISTS

Number of states or part of states involved in the Louisiana Purchase?
4. THIRTEEN
5. MISSOURI

Two states involved in a compromise (5, 6)
6. MAINE

...AND AT THE SAME TIME

From where and to where did the Savannah sail? **Savannah, GA to Liverpool, England**

Page 5

John Quincy Adams

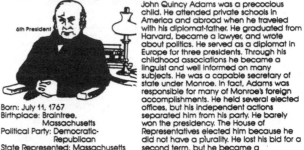

6th President

Name _____

John Quincy Adams was a precocious child. He attended private schools in America and abroad when he traveled with his diplomat-father. He graduated from Harvard, became a lawyer, and wrote about politics. He served as a diplomat in Europe for three presidents. Through his childhood associations he became a linguist and well informed on many subjects. He was a capable secretary of state under Monroe. In fact, Adams was responsible for many of Monroe's foreign accomplishments. He held several elected offices, but his independent actions separated him from his party. He barely won the presidency. The House of Representatives elected him because he did not have a plurality. He lost his bid for a second term, but he became a representative in Congress where he argued strongly for what he believed, no matter how controversial. In fact, he had a stroke debating an issue and died two days later.

Born: July 11, 1767
Birthplace: Braintree, Massachusetts
Political Party: Democratic-Republican
State Represented: Massachusetts
Term: March 4, 1825–March 3, 1829
Died: February 23, 1848
Vice President: John Caldwell Calhoun (DR)

DISCOVER FOR YOURSELF

Across
1. First party to which J.Q. Adams belonged
3. His home
5. Name of treaty signed after War of 1812
7. Last party to which he belonged
8. The man who received more electoral votes in 1824

Down
1. Number of children
2. Institution he established; still in Washington, D.C.
4. The man who made it possible to win the presidency in 1824
6. Wife's name

...AND AT THE SAME TIME

What did Hans Oersted discover around 1820? **electricity produces magnetism**

Page 6

Andrew Jackson

"Our Federal Union: it must be preserved."

7th President

Name _____

Andrew Jackson was the first president born in a log cabin. He had no male adult to look up to as his father died before he was born. Jackson was self-made. He went to school until he was thirteen. Then he fought in the Revolutionary War. The scar on his forehead came when he refused to obey his captors. He had a reputation of being tough and was nicknamed "Old Hickory". In spite of his limited education, he became a lawyer and politician in what was to be Tennessee. He became a national hero in the War of 1812. His military fame helped him win the presidency. He was the first president to be elected by the people. Opponents dubbed his supporters "the mob". He was a strong leader. He used the powers of the presidency to veto and argue with Congress for the benefit of the working man. He fought for the preservation of the Union.

Born: March 15, 1767
Birthplace: Waxhaw District, South Carolina
Political Party: Democratic
State Represented: Tennessee
Term: March 4, 1829–March 3, 1837
Died: June 8, 1845
Vice President: John Calhoun (D)
Martin Van Buren (D)

DISCOVER FOR YOURSELF

Find the letters that spell the names of the four Indian tribes that were moved west of the Mississippi. Cross them out as you write them in the lines below.

Creek, Cherokee, Choctaw, Chickasaw

Find the letters that spell the name of the one tribe that did not move. Write its name on the line below.

Seminole

The letters that remain will spell Jackson's slogan. Unscramble the letters and write his slogan. (4 words) **Let the People Rule**

...AND AT THE SAME TIME

What did Michael Faraday discover? **electromagnetism**

Page 7

Martin Van Buren

8th President

Name _____

Martin Van Buren was the son of a truck farmer-innkeeper father. He met politicians who stopped by the inn on their way to and from the state capital. He became a law clerk at age fourteen after attending a village school. By twenty-one he had a successful law practice. He was ambitious as a politician. He was nicknamed "Little Magician" because of his political prowess and his small size. Helped Andrew Jackson win the presidency, and as a reward Jackson appointed him secretary of state and then vice president. In 1836, Van Buren was elected president. Soon after, the nation suffered a depression. Van Buren's popularity decreased because of the financial panic, border disputes and accusations from pro-slavery and anti-slavery leaders. He was defeated in his bid for a second term and a third time in 1848 when he ran on the Free Soil Party ticket—a group opposed to slavery.

Born: December 5, 1782
Birthplace: Kinderhook, New York
Political Party: Democratic
State Represented: New York
Term: March 4, 1837–March 3, 1841
Died: July 24, 1862
Vice President: Richard Johnson (D)

DISCOVER FOR YOURSELF

Fill in the time line with either the date or the event.

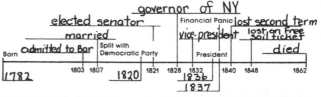

governor of NY
elected senator | Financial Panic | lost second term
married | vice-president | lost on Free soil ticket
Born | admitted to Bar | Split with Democratic Party | President | died

1782 | 1803 | 1807 | 1820 | 1821 | 1828 | 1832 | 1836/1837 | 1840 | 1848 | 1862

...AND AT THE SAME TIME

Who became the monarch of England in 1838 and for how long? **Queen Victoria 63 years**

Page 8

Answer Key

William H. Harrison

Name _____

9th President

William Henry Harrison was a descendent of a prominent Virginia family. His early schooling was at home. He left college before graduation to study medicine. When his father died, he joined the army. After seven years of a military career he entered politics. As governor of the Indiana Territory he was victorious against the Indians at the Battle of Tippecanoe, and again showed his military skill in the War of 1812. After that war he resigned again from military life. He ran his farm, was a state and U.S. senator and a diplomat. He was unsuccessful in 1836 in his bid for the presidency, but in 1840 he won on the slogan "Tippecanoe and Tyler too". He caught cold at his inauguration. It turned into pneumonia and he died after only thirty-two days in office. He was not president long enough to put any programs into effect, so it is difficult to say if he was successful as president.

Born: February 9, 1773
Birthplace: Berkely, Charles City County, Virginia
Political Party: Whig
State Represented: Ohio
Term: March 4, 1841–April 4, 1841
Died: April 4, 1841
Vice President: John Tyler (W)

DISCOVER FOR YOURSELF

Mark the following statements true or false.

__F__ Harrison never went to college.

__F__ Seventy-three electoral votes were enough to win the presidency then.

__F__ He received the name Tippecanoe because he had an accident in a boat.

__T__ He served as Secretary to the Northwest Territory.

__T__ Harrison ran for president more than once.

__T__ He served the shortest time in office of any president.

...AND AT THE SAME TIME

Charles Dickens was an English author. He wrote many books at this time. Name two of them. __Answers will vary.__

John Tyler

Name _____

10th President

John Tyler was the son of a distinguished plantation family. He went to private school and William and Mary College. Upon graduation he studied law with his father. He entered politics and held state and national offices. He had been a Democratic-Republican but became a Whig. When Harrison died Tyler found himself without a party because he could not agree with the Whig legislators.* He had opposing views about national banks, tariffs, federally financed projects and slavery. In spite of these differences he passed settlement laws, established trade with China, ended the second Seminole War, and paved the way for Texas' annexation. Above all, he established the presidency as a full-powered position when reached as a result of the president's death. At the end of the term he retired from politics until 1860 when he voted in favor of Virginia's leaving the Union at the state secession convention.

Born: March 29, 1790
Birthplace: Charles City County, Virginia
Political Party: Whig (D/R)*
State Represented: Virginia
Term: April 6, 1841–March 3, 1845
Died: January 18, 1862
Vice President: vacant

DISCOVER FOR YOURSELF

Fill in the blanks.

The __Whig__ Party was comprised of several groups with no agreed upon policies.

Tyler __vetoed__ many of Congress' bills.

His __daughter__ was his White House hostess until he married __Julia Gardiner__, his second wife.

His party disagreements were so strong that some Whigs tried to __impeach__ him.

After fighting with the __Seminole__ Indians ended, __Florida__ became a state.

__Sherwood Forest__ is the name of his estate.

...AND AT THE SAME TIME

What did the message Morse tapped out in 1844 say? __What hath God wrought!__

James K. Polk

Name _____

11th President

James Polk was the eldest of ten children. He was sickly and therefore spared doing his share of farm chores. Although he had little formal education, he was studious and after graduating from the University of North Carolina he studied law. Politics proved more exciting than practicing law, and soon Polk was involved in state and then national politics. He was nominated at the Democratic Presidential Convention on the ninth ballot. He was the first "Dark Horse" candidate to run and then win the presidency. During his tenure America had its largest growth. He guided the nation through the Mexican War and settled the Oregon boundary. He was able to complete the program he outlined during the campaign—something few presidents are able to do. He kept his campaign promise and did not seek a second term.

Born: November 2, 1795
Birthplace: Near Pineville, Mecklenburg County, North Carolina
Political Party: Democratic
State Represented: Tennessee
Term: March 4, 1845–March 3, 1849
Died: June 15, 1849
Vice President: George Dallas (D)

DISCOVER FOR YOURSELF

Fill in the answer to each clue on the lines to the right. Add up the numbers under every letter A to discover what Polk's age was when he became president.

The name of his home

P o l k   P l a c e
1 5 2 6   4 7 9 8 3

A friend of the family and a man Polk supported as president

J a c k s o n
2 5 5 3 6 1 4

Wife's name

S a r a h
9 8 2 6 4

His opponent for president

H e n r y   C l a y
4 5 7 1 9   1 5 7 3

Country with whom he settled Oregon boundary

B r i t a i n
1 6 3 4 5 7 2

Original family name

P o l l a c k
8 3 7 4 9 5 6

He was __49__ years old when he became president.

...AND AT THE SAME TIME

What did William Morton do in 1846? __demonstrated ether__

Zachary Taylor

Name _____

12th President

Zachary Taylor was raised near the Kentucky frontier on the family farm. There were no schools, so he studied with tutors. He joined the army in his teens and had a military career for forty years. He fought in many battles and became a hero. The Whig Party recognized his popularity and drafted him as their nominee. He was the first military leader to become president without holding a political office previously. He realized he lacked experience so he sought advice from others, but his decisions were always based on his perception of each situation. Slavery and the extension of slavery in the newly acquired western land were the main issues of his term. They were never resolved however, because he died suddenly after only sixteen months in office.

Born: November 24, 1784
Birthplace: Montebello, Orange County, Virginia
Political Party: Whig
State Represented: Louisiana
Term: March 4, 1849–July 9, 1850
Died: July 9, 1850
Vice President: Millard Fillmore (W)

DISCOVER FOR YOURSELF

What day of the week was Taylor inaugurated? __Monday__

What was his nickname? __Old Rough and Ready__

What was happening in California at the time of Taylor's term? __Gold Rush__

Who was his private secretary and what was the relation? __William Bliss, his son-in-law__

With what country was the Clayton-Bulwer Treaty signed? __England__

Why did President Polk send General Scott to lead the army into Mexico rather than Taylor? __Taylor was getting too popular.__

...AND AT THE SAME TIME

Who discovered gold first and where in California? __James Wilson Marshall at Sutter's Mill__

 IF8750 U.S. Government

Answer Key

Millard Fillmore

13th President

Name _____

Millard Fillmore was born in a log cabin. He had a limited elementary school education. When he was fourteen he became an apprentice to a clothmaker until he decided to study law. He was elected to several state offices and to the U.S. House of Representatives. He succeeded to the presidency after Zachary Taylor's death. Fillmore delayed the Civil War with passage of the Compromise of 1850. He worked for the expansion of the U.S. railroads, sent Commodore Matthew C. Perry to Japan to establish trade and diplomatic relations, and reduced the five cent stamp to three cents. The Whig Party was angry about his attitude toward slavery. They did not renominate him. He returned to Buffalo and resumed his law practice. He was nominated in 1856 for president but lost. He lived out his life as a philanthropic citizen in Buffalo.

Born: January 7, 1800
Birthplace: Summerhill, Cayuga County, New York
Political Party: Whig
State Represented: New York
Term: July 10, 1850–March 3, 1853
Died: March 8, 1874
Vice President: vacant

DISCOVER FOR YOURSELF

The names of the two parties that nominated Millard Fillmore are hidden in the puzzle to the right. Start in the box where the arrow is pointing. Move from letter to letter in any direction without jumping a letter. What are the names of the two parties that nominated him?

<u>The Know-Nothing and</u>
<u>Whig Parties</u>

...AND AT THE SAME TIME
Who was the Emperor of France in 1852? <u>Napoleon III</u>

Page 13

Franklin Pierce

14th President

Name _____

Franklin Pierce was the son of a farmer, innkeeper, militia leader and politician. He went to a local school until age eleven. Then he attended private schools and Bowdoin College. He studied law and practiced law between holding elected state and national offices. During the Mexican War he enlisted in the army. After the war he resumed his law practice until he was nominated for president on the forty-ninth ballot. He was the youngest president to take office. He became unpopular with the signing of a bill that allowed Kansas and Nebraska settlers to vote whether they wanted slavery, in his quest for Cuba, and his sponsorship of a southern transcontinental railroad. The Democratic Party rejected him for a second term. He returned to New Hampshire full of bitterness. Even his community scorned him for his views on slavery.

Born: November 23, 1804
Birthplace: Hillsborough, New Hampshire
Political Party: Democratic
State Represented: New Hampshire
Term: March 4, 1853–March 3, 1857
Died: October 8, 1869
Vice President: William King (D)

DISCOVER FOR YOURSELF
Write the answer to each clue or question in the row of boxes to the right. Rearrange the circled letters on the line below to tell what the people in Washington called Mrs. Pierce.

What state nominated Pierce for president? `V I R G I N I A`

Who was Mrs. Abby Kent Means? `WHITE HOUSE HOSTESS`

Pierce's presidential opponent `WINFIELD SCOTT`
When had Pierce worked for him? `THE MEXICAN WAR`

Pierce's home town `CONCORD`
What Washington called Mrs. Pierce <u>Shadow of the White House</u>

...AND AT THE SAME TIME
What did Johan Lundstrom invent and manufacture in 1855? <u>safety match</u>

Page 14

James Buchanan

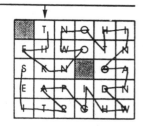

15th President

Name _____

James Buchanan was born in a log cabin. His father ran a store. Buchanan learned arithmetic while helping in the store and Greek and Latin from the pastor. He graduated from college in 1809 and studied law. He had a good law practice and success in business due in part to his early training. After the time he spent as a volunteer soldier in the War of 1812, he spent the rest of his life in public service. Because he was on diplomatic assignments abroad, his feelings about slavery were not known which made him an acceptable candidate for president. In spite of his diplomatic skill, he was not able to mend the wounds made before his administration. Neither the northern or southern party chose him as a candidate in 1860. After Lincoln was elected, but not yet inaugurated, seven states seceded from the Union and set up the Confederate States. Buchanan retired to his house in Pennsylvania, but remained a supporter of the Union.

Born: April 23, 1791
Birthplace: Cove Gap, Pennsylvania
Political Party: Democratic
State Represented: Pennsylvania
Term: March 4, 1857–March 3, 1861
Died: June 1, 1868
Vice President: John Breckinridge (D)

DISCOVER FOR YOURSELF
Write the answers to each clue in the row of boxes following. The number in the boxes where the letter A falls will add up to the number of electoral votes by which Buchanan beat his opponent.

Name of his home <u>W h e a t l a n d</u>
  3 5 4 8 2 9 7 1 6

Name of first state to secede <u>S o u t h C a r o l i n a</u>
  10 6 7 5 8   1 8 9 7 3 4 5 9

Country where he held first diplomatic assignment <u>R u s s i a</u>
  6 1 8 4 1 7

First Confederate State's president <u>J e f f e r s o n D a v i s</u>
  1 7 10 6 9 8 4 5 8   3 8 2 9 6

Man who lost election to him <u>F r e m o n t</u>
  10 3 7 9 8 5 1

Buchanan's hostess <u>H a r r i e t L a n e</u>
  1 7 8 5 9 6 2   4 6 7 3

By how many electoral votes did he win? <u>60</u>

...AND AT THE SAME TIME
Why did the Pony Express last only a year and a half? <u>coast to coast telegraph completed</u>

Page 15

Abraham Lincoln

16th President

Name _____

Abraham Lincoln's father, a farmer and carpenter, was unable to read or write. Lincoln was self taught as he had less than a year of formal education. He had many jobs, was postmaster of New Salem, and won a seat in the state legislature before completing his study of law. He rode the circuit on horseback trying cases before entering national politics. As a representative to Congress he was against slavery in new territory, but felt the government should not interfere with it where it already existed. In 1856 he joined the Republican Party, an antislavery coalition. He ran against Stephen Douglas for senate. Although he lost, Lincoln became well-known through their debates. Lincoln inherited a tense situation when he became president. War soon broke out. He was shot a few weeks after the start of his second term and never was able to carry out his postwar policies.

Born: February 12, 1809
Birthplace: Hardin County, Kentucky
Political Party: Republican
State Represented: Illinois
Term: March 4, 1861–April 15, 1865
Died: April 15, 1865
Vice President: (1) Hannibal Hamlin (R)
                (2) Andrew Johnson (D)

DISCOVER FOR YOURSELF
Name several jobs he held as a young man. <u>Answers may vary: clerk, railsplitter, deck hand, millhand, handyman</u>

In what speech did he say, "malice toward none, with charity for all"? <u>Second Inaugural Address</u>

What battle started the Civil War? <u>Fort Sumter</u>

Why and when was the Gettysburg Address delivered? <u>11/19/1863 - to dedicate cemetery</u>

What proclamation declared freedom for slaves? <u>Emancipation Proclamation</u>

This proclamation was the basis for what Amendment to the Constitution? <u>13</u>

How did Lincoln travel to the White House for his inauguration? <u>by train</u>

On what ticket was he elected the second time? <u>National Union Party</u>

...AND AT THE SAME TIME
How were people able to communicate with one another over great distances? <u>Answers may vary: Pony Express, telegraph, newspapers</u>

Page 16

Answer Key

Andrew Johnson

Name _____

17th President

Andrew Johnson taught himself to read, but his wife was responsible for most of his education. His father died early, and he worked in the tailoring profession. He was somewhat successful in business and became active in local and national politics. He favored the common man. He voted independent of his party and the South from where he came. He was the only southern senator to stay in Washington after his state seceded. Lincoln chose him as his running mate on the National Union Party's ticket. Upon Lincoln's death, the job of Reconstruction befell Johnson. He offered a pardon to all southerners who were not military leaders or officials and brought the seceded states back into the Union. Radicals disapproved. He was impeached but missed conviction by one vote. He remained active in politics after his presidency, and was applauded when he returned to Washington as a senator.

Born: December 29, 1808
Birthplace: Raleigh, North Carolina
Political Party: Democratic
State Represented: Tennessee
Term: April 15, 1865–March 3, 1869
Died: July 31, 1875
Vice President: vacant

DISCOVER FOR YOURSELF

Mark the following statements true or false.

_F_ Johnson was impeached and convicted by one vote.

_F_ Austria occupied Mexico in 1865.

_T_ Alaska was purchased from Russia.

_T_ Stanton was dismissed for being too radical.

_F_ Edwin Stanton was Secretary of State.

_T_ The purchase of Alaska was called "Seward's Folly".

_F_ Johnson died in the senate.

_F_ Dynamite was used in the Civil War.

...AND AT THE SAME TIME

Name a French chemist who discovered diseases come from germs. Louis Pasteur

Page 17

Ulysses S. Grant

Name _____

18th President

Ulysses Grant did not like helping on his father's farm or tannery. His only real fondness was for horses. After graduation from West Point, he served in the Army for several years. After the Mexican War, he left the service and tried to support his family by farming and in business, but he was a failure. He rejoined the Army when the Civil War began. He was put in charge of the Union armies. At the end of the war he was a hero in the North, and the South appreciated his treatment of General Lee. Grant had never associated with a political party, but he seemed to favor the Republicans. They nominated him for president, and he won easily. Some of his appointees were not honest. His able military leadership did not carry over to the presidency. In fact, his family might have been penniless had he not finished his autobiography a few days before he died.

Born: April 27, 1822
Birthplace: Point Pleasant, Ohio
Political Party: Republican
State Represented: Illinois
Term: March 4, 1869–March 3, 1877
Died: July 23, 1885
Vice President: (1) Schuyler Colfax (R)
(2) Henry Wilson (R)

DISCOVER FOR YOURSELF

Write the answer to each clue in the row of boxes to the right. Rearrange the circled letters on the lines below to tell the name of the cabin he built near St. Louis.

A confederate warship — A L A B A M A

Grant's real first name — H I R A M

Where he first lived with his wife — S T L O U I S

Some people called him this because he had so many casualties in the war — B U T C H E R

His wife's name — J U L I A D E N T

The name of the cabin near St. Louis was Hardscrabble

...AND AT THE SAME TIME

What happened in Promontory, Utah on May 10th 1869? Transcontinental railroad complete

Page 18

Rutherford Hayes

Name _____

19th President

A bachelor uncle served as Rutherford Hayes' guardian because his father died before he was born. Hayes received a good education. He was a successful criminal lawyer until he became a soldier during the Civil War. He was elected to Congress while still fighting, but he would not take his seat until the war ended. After being elected governor of Ohio three times, the Republican Party nominated him for the presidency. The election was close. A special commission had to settle it. Hayes won by one electoral vote. He ended Reconstruction, tried to appoint qualified personnel, and sent troops in where strikers caused riots. He left office at the end of one term as he had promised. He returned to Ohio where he was active in several humanitarian causes until his death.

Born: October 4, 1822
Birthplace: Delaware, Ohio
Political Party: Republican
State Represented: Ohio
Term: March 4, 1877–March 3, 1881
Died: January 17, 1893
Vice President: William Wheeler (R)

DISCOVER FOR YOURSELF

The motto by which Hayes lived is hidden in the puzzle to the right. Start in the box where the arrow is pointing. Move from letter to letter in any direction without jumping a letter. Write his motto on the lines below.

H	A	R	T	E	S	W	H
V	E	E	P	S	V	B	O
E	R	S	I	O	S	E	S
T	S	H	R	U	C	R	E
S	E	B	Y	T	N	H	B

He serves his party best who serves his country best

...AND AT THE SAME TIME

List three inventions of the time. phonograph, phone, street lights

Page 19

James A. Garfield

Name _____

20th President

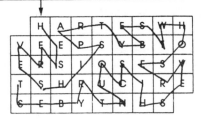

James Garfield received a good education even though he had to work hard on the family farm at odd jobs to earn money. He graduated from college, taught and studied law. He fought in the Civil War. He had shown an interest in politics before the war and was elected to the U.S. House of Representatives while still in the Army. He served nine terms in Congress. During this time he was accused of accepting "gifts" illegally, but it was never proven. In 1880, he was nominated for president on the thirty-sixth ballot. As president, he awarded several appointments in return for favors received. A disappointed office seeker shot him. He lived eighty days after the shooting. Because of his death, Congress began immediately to get rid of the "spoils system" and install a civil service system.

Born: November 19, 1831
Birthplace: Orange, Ohio
Political Party: Republican
State Represented: Ohio
Term: March 4, 1881–September 19, 1881
Died: September 19, 1881
Vice President: Chester Arthur (R)

DISCOVER FOR YOURSELF

Mark the following statements true or false.

_T_ If X-ray had existed, Garfield may have lived.

_T_ Garfield's mother saw him inaugurated.

_F_ Garfield ran against John Fremont.

_F_ He ran on the Half-Breed ticket for president.

_T_ Some of Garfield's children served other presidents.

_T_ Garfield was very intelligent.

_T_ He was shot on July 2, 1881.

_F_ He was a sailor as a young man.

_F_ He supported Andrew Johnson.

...AND AT THE SAME TIME

Clara Barton founded the American Red Cross. What had she done before? Nurse in Civil War

Page 20

Answer Key

Chester A. Arthur
21st President

Name _____

Chester Arthur attended many local schools because his father's pastoral duties required the family move a lot. After college he studied law and became a defender of civil rights for blacks. He became involved with the start of the Republican Party and accepted political assignments for favors done. He was in the state militia in administrative positions during the Civil War. After the war he returned to practicing law and Republican politics. He was nominated as Garfield's running mate because of his strong party loyalty. Much to the surprise of party leaders, when Arthur succeeded to the presidency, he did not make political appointments. In fact, he signed the Civil Service Act. Arthur knew he had a fatal illness which he kept a secret. After completing the term he retired to New York.

Born: October 5, 1829
Birthplace: Fairfield, Vermont
Political Party: Republican
State Represented: New York
Term: September 20, 1881–March 3, 1885
Died: November 18, 1886
Vice President: vacant

DISCOVER FOR YOURSELF
Circle the hidden words in the puzzle that answer the clues below. Words in the puzzle appear forward, backward or diagonally. Write the answer to each clue on the line next to or under it.

```
O G A C I H C N
G O N T H R E E
Y T R H A U N D
E L L E N A V Y
N A Y I T H E D
D S O S H S T I
I N E Y A V I K
K C O C N A H S
```

The first skyscraper was built in this city __Chicago__

Wife's name __Ellen__

College name __Union__

His hostess __sister__

Who the Garfield/ Arthur ticket defeated __Hancock__

Branch of service he modernized __Navy__

Number of children he had __three__

...AND AT THE SAME TIME
What was Mark Twain's real name? __Samuel Clemens__

Page 21

Grover Cleveland
22nd President - 24th President

Name _____

Grover Cleveland attended local schools until he was fourteen. Then he had to work to help support the family. He studied law and entered politics as a party worker. He worked his way up through local and state offices. His honesty and hard work earned him the Democratic nomination for president in 1884. A name-calling campaign ensued. Cleveland was the first Democrat elected since the Civil War. He did serve a second term, but not consecutively. He lost in 1888 but was elected four years later. Financial depression and labor problems filled his second term. He was not able to solve all the problems. He did not seek a third term. In his retirement he was a college lecturer and author and eventually regained the respect he had earned.

Born: March 18, 1837
Birthplace: Caldwell, New Jersey
Political Party: Democratic
State Represented: New York
Terms: March 4, 1885–March 3, 1889
      March 4, 1893–March 3, 1897
Died: June 24, 1908
Vice President: (1) Thomas Hendricks (D)
               (2) Adlai Stevenson (D)

DISCOVER FOR YOURSELF
Fill in the answer to each clue on the lines to the right.

The name he dropped as a boy __Stephen__

What young relatives called him __Uncle Jumbo__

What Republicans who supported Cleveland were called __Mugwumps__

The currency of the day __Gold__

Person that defeated him in 1888 __Harrison__

This VP has a relative in Illinois that is in politics now. __Stevenson__

Cleveland was the only president to marry in the White House. Name his bride. __Frances Folsom__

Where he lectured __Princeton__

Fill in the letters whose number matches those under the lines below to learn what he said on his death bed.
__I have tried so hard to do right__

...AND AT THE SAME TIME
Why did France give the Statue of Liberty to the U.S.? __friendly gesture__

Page 22

Benjamin Harrison
23rd President

Name _____

Benjamin Harrison was the descendent of a patriotic family. His early education was with tutors. After college he studied law and became a prominent lawyer. He began to work for the Republican Party. After the Civil War he became interested in holding office. By 1888 he had become known because of his name, and as a soldier, lawyer and politician. The Republicans nominated him for president. He did not win the popular vote, but he did win the electoral vote. He was strong in foreign affairs. He built a two-ocean navy, negotiated trade policies, and created the Pan American Union. He let domestic affairs follow party lines and congressional leadership. His attitude toward taxes, pensions and trusts probably cost him the election in 1892. He practiced law and wrote until his death in his home in Indiana.

Born: August 20, 1833
Birthplace: North Bend, Ohio
Political Party: Republican
State Represented: Indiana
Term: March 4, 1889–March 3, 1893
Died: March 13, 1901
Vice President: Levi P. Morton (R)

DISCOVER FOR YOURSELF

Find the letters that spell the names of the states that joined the Union during Harrison's term. Cross them out as you write them on the lines below.
__North Dakota, South Dakota, Washington, Wyoming, Montana__

The letters that remain will spell the name of a campaign song. Unscramble the letters and write the name of the song. (4 words) __Grandfather's hat fits Ben__

...AND AT THE SAME TIME
Where was basketball first played? __Springfield, MA.__

Page 23

William McKinley
25th President

Name _____

William McKinley went to local and private schools before entering college. After serving in the Civil War he studied law. At an early age he knew he wanted to be president. He held local, state and national offices. He would not travel during the presidential campaign because of his invalid wife, so crowds traveled to hear him speak from his front porch. He had the first popular vote majority since 1872. During his term the Spanish-American War was fought. The U.S. obtained Guam, Puerto Rico and the Philippines in the peace settlement. Domestically he was for higher tariffs and the gold standard. Six months after his second term began, he was shot by an anarchist. He died nine days later.

Born: January 29, 1843
Birthplace: Niles, Ohio
Political Party: Republican
State Represented: Ohio
Term: March 4, 1897–September 14, 1901
Died: September 14, 1901
Vice President: (1) Garret Hobart (R)
               (2) Theodore Roosevelt (R)

DISCOVER FOR YOURSELF
Write the answer to each clue in the row of boxes to the right. Rearrange the circled letters on the lines below to tell one of his campaign promises.

Slogan that began the war
__REMEMBER THE MAINE__

Mrs. McKinley suffered with this disease: __EPILEPSY__

The country that gained independence after the Spanish-American War __CUBA__

This man lost to McKinley two times.
__WILLIAM JENNINGS BRYAN__

The campaign promise he made means they would have this: __FOOD__

Write the promise he made to the voters. __Full dinner pail__

...AND AT THE SAME TIME
Who discovered the gold in the Klondike? __George Carmack and his Indian wife__

Page 24

Answer Key

Theodore Roosevelt

26th President

Theodore Roosevelt was an energetic yet frail child with a curious mind. He had private tutors until he went to Harvard. Being a lawyer did not interest him but public service did. He was elected to the state legislature at twenty-three. He turned to ranching and writing for a while after his first wife and mother died. He held several appointed offices upon his return to politics. He became a hero as commander of the Rough Riders in the Spanish-American War and was elected governor of New York. The Party did not like the way he ran the state so they ran him for vice president to get rid of him. Six months after the election he was president. Among his many accomplishments was the start of the Panama Canal. He was a conservationist. He was considered a progressive. He did not seek a third term in 1908, but he did run in 1912 and lost. He was involved with politics until the day he died.

Born: October 27, 1858
Birthplace: New York, New York
Political Party: Republican
State Represented: New York
Term: September 14, 1901–March 3, 1909
Died: January 6, 1919
Vice President: (1) vacant
(2) Charles Fairbanks (R)

DISCOVER FOR YOURSELF
Write the answer to each clue in the row of boxes to the right. There will be two words that form vertically. They will be the two missing words from a famous phrase he spoke: "Speak softly and carry a **Big Stick**. You will go far."

What Roosevelt won as peace mediator — NOBEL PRIZE
U.S. Warships that made world tour — GREAT WHITE FLEET
Disease he caught in Brazil — JUNGLE FEVER
Party ticket in 1912 — BULL MOOSE
What his kids were called in White House — WHITE HOUSE GANG
His home in New York — SAGAMORE HILL
Group he played tennis with — TENNIS CABINET
The president before him — MCKINLEY
Write the surprise words in the blanks above.

...AND AT THE SAME TIME
He wrote Up from Slavery and was an advisor to Roosevelt. **Booker T. Washington**

Page 25

William H. Taft

27th President

William Taft was a descendant of early settlers in America and a Republican family. He was well educated. He spent twenty years of his life as a judge and practicing law. He held only one elected office before the presidency. All others were appointed. When Roosevelt announced he would not seek another term, he hand-picked Taft. Taft won by over a million votes. He had some Party differences and was not the aggressive administrator Roosevelt had been. Roosevelt did not like the way Taft was handling big business and conservation matters so he decided to run again on the Bull Moose ticket. They both lost. Taft returned to his law practice, taught and engaged in philanthropic activities until he was appointed as Chief Justice of the Supreme Court in 1921. He finally reached his life's ambition.

Born: September 15, 1857
Birthplace: Cincinnati, Ohio
Political Party: Republican
State Represented: Ohio
Term: March 4, 1909–March 3, 1913
Died: March 8, 1930
Vice President: James Sherman (R)

DISCOVER FOR YOURSELF
Across
4. Custom he established in spring of each year (2 words)
5. President who made him Chief Justice
8. What he said the White House was
9. His Secretary of State

Down
1. Where he was governor
2. Number of electoral votes in 1912
3. Weather on inauguration
6. What Amendment 16 levies (2 words)
7. Brothers and sisters' nickname for him (2 words)

...AND AT THE SAME TIME
What two areas were discovered (1909 and 1911) and by whom? **North and South Poles by Perry and Amundsen**

Page 26

Woodrow Wilson

28th President

Woodrow Wilson's family was a religious one and valued a good education. He was taught at home until he was nine because the war had closed many schools. Wilson studied law but decided he liked teaching. As president of Princeton he emerged as a man for the masses and honest—a perfect candidate for governor of New York. He was a reformer and used the governorship as a stepping stone to the presidency. He won that nomination on the forty-sixth ballot. He won the election because of the split Republican ticket. He fought for the people and aggressively pursued his idealistic views. That, along with keeping the nation out of war, won Wilson a second term. However, three months later the U.S. was at war. After the war, he worked for peace. He suffered a stroke while still in office, but he did not give up the presidency. He died three years after leaving the White House.

Born: December 29, 1856
Birthplace: Staunton, Virginia
Political Party: Democratic
State Represented: New Jersey
Term: March 4, 1913–March 3, 1921
Died: February 3, 1924
Vice President: Thomas Marshall (D)

DISCOVER FOR YOURSELF
By what name was he called as a child? **Tommy**
For what college was he president? **Princeton**
What war was being fought when he was a boy? **Civil War**
When did he say, "Let the people come forward"? **Inauguration Address**
What act did he sign into law that set up the U.S. central banking system used today? **Federal Reserve Act**
What war was fought during his administration? **World War I**
For what cause was he fighting when he had his stroke? **League of Nations membership**
Where is he buried? **Washington D.C.**

...AND AT THE SAME TIME
What was the Lusitania and what happened to it? **passenger ship torpedoed by Germans**

Page 27

Warren G. Harding

29th President

Warren Harding attended school, taught, read law and sold insurance before he settled on publishing. Through his journalistic work he became known in the state and was elected to state senator, lieutenant governor and U.S. senator. He worked his way through Party ranks and was nominated for the presidency in 1920. He relied on his cabinet and Congress for leadership. Some of his appointments proved to be corrupt and used their offices for personal gain. When the scams were revealed, cabinet members and friends were sent to jail and committed suicide. In an effort to regain confidence in his administration, Harding made a trip by train across the country. He became ill on the trip and died. The exact cause is not known. His wife burned as many of his papers as she could to protect his name.

Born: November 2, 1865
Birthplace: Corsica, Ohio
Political Party: Republican
State Represented: Ohio
Term: March 4, 1921–August 2, 1923
Died: August 2, 1923
Vice President: Calvin Coolidge (D)

DISCOVER FOR YOURSELF
Fill in the blanks.
The **Teapot Dome** involved leasing government-owned oil reserves to private companies.
Daugherty was Harding's political sponsor.
Harding brought so many of his friends to Washington, that they were called the **Ohio Gang**.
Harding died in **San Francisco**.
The 1920 election was the first time **women** were allowed to vote.
A **radio** broadcast the results of the election for the first time in 1920.
When the nominating convention was deadlocked, they nominated Harding as the **compromise** candidate.

...AND AT THE SAME TIME
What automobile manufacturer sold the most cars in 1921? **Ford**

Page 28

Answer Key

Calvin Coolidge

30th President

Name _____

Calvin Coolidge was educated in public and private schools before entering Amherst College. After college he studied law and soon became active in politics, following in his father's footsteps. He held many local and state offices before being recognized nationally. He was the opposite of outgoing Harding. He earned the name "Silent Sam" because he was a man of few words and seldom smiled. He was the first vice president to attend cabinet meetings. When Harding died, Coolidge was awakened at his father's farm. After dressing, he was sworn in by his father, and then went back to bed. Coolidge cleaned up the scandals of Harding's administration. He was honest and frugal. He won the 1924 election in his own right using the slogan "Keep Cool with Coolidge". He chose not to run in 1928 and said, "Good-bye, I have had a very nice time in Washington."

Born: July 4, 1872
Birthplace: Plymouth, Vermont
Political Party: Republican
State Represented: Massachusetts
Term: August 3, 1923–March 3, 1929
Died: January 5, 1933
Vice President: (1) vacant
         (2) Charles Dawes III (R)

DISCOVER FOR YOURSELF

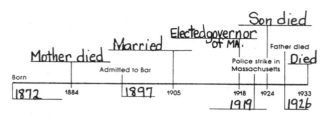

Mother died — *Born* — 1872 — 1884 — Admitted to Bar — Married — 1897 — 1905 — Elected governor of MA. — Police strike in Massachusetts — 1918 — 1919 — 1924 — Son died — Father died — Died — 1933 — 1926

...AND AT THE SAME TIME

Where were the first Winter Olympics held and in what year?
1924—Chamonix, France

Page 29

Herbert C. Hoover

31st President

Name _____

Herbert Hoover's parents were dead by the time he was nine. He was raised by several relatives and had a sporadic early education. His college degree was in geology and mining engineering. He made a fortune developing mines all over the world. He served in the administrations of Wilson, Harding and Coolidge. He was a highly organized administrator as head of the U.S. Food Administration and Secretary of Commerce. His skills were recognized by the Republican Party and he was nominated for president in 1928. He won in a landslide victory, but lost the same way in 1932—probably due to his inability to stop the Depression that hit seven months after he took office. He had many active years after his term as an author, humanitarian and advisor to two presidents. He gave the money he made from the government jobs to charitable projects.

Born: August 10, 1874
Birthplace: West Branch, Iowa
Political Party: Republican
State Represented: California
Term: March 4, 1929–March 3, 1933
Died: October 20, 1964
Vice President: Charles Curtis (R)

DISCOVER FOR YOURSELF

Circle the hidden words in the puzzle that answer the clues below. Answers appear forward, backward, up, down or diagonally. Write the answer to each clue on the line next to or under it.

Where he went to college Stanford

Troops from this country invaded Manchuria Japan

Hoover's 1928 opponent (2 words) Al Smith

Hoover's wife's name (2 words) Lou Henry

He was last of this type president.(2 words) Lame Duck

Hoover was this by the age of nine Orphan

```
K C U D E M A L
L A D H M E O I
I L R U A U R A
E V O O H H P N
R L F E C O H E
U O N N A P A J
R R A J A P N A
Y M T A N F R D
A L S M I T H O
```

...AND AT THE SAME TIME

When were the first Academy Awards held and what was the best film? May 1929 "Wings"

Page 30

Franklin D. Roosevelt

32nd President

Name _____

Franklin Roosevelt was born into a wealthy family. He had tutors or went to private schools and traveled in Europe with his family. After Harvard he studied law, but decided politics was what he wanted. He won some and lost some elections, but he was a fighter as was proven when he was struck with polio. He refused to give up and was elected president eleven years later. The words he spoke at his inauguration, "The only thing we have to fear is fear itself" gave the people confidence in his ability to lead them. He led the country through two huge "battles": the Depression and World War II (the end of which he did not see). He had more accomplishments—far too many to list. He was elected to three more terms. No other president ever has or ever will serve that many again. He died about three months after the start of his fourth term.

Born: January 30, 1882
Birthplace: Hyde Park, New York
Political Party: Democratic
State Represented: New York
Term: March 4, 1933–April 12, 1945
Died: April 12, 1945
Vice President: (1) John Garner (D)
         (2) John Garner (D)
         (3) Henry Wallace (D)
         (4) Harry Truman (D)

DISCOVER FOR YOURSELF

Across
1. Man killed in assassination attempt instead of Roosevelt
3. Number of children he had
6. What his "talks" on radio were called (2 words)
8. The event in 1941 that brought U.S. into the war (2 words)
9. World War II actually began when Germany invaded this country in 1939

Down
1. T. Roosevelt and F. Roosevelt were this
2. What the enemy was called
4. What Roosevelt called his program
5. What Franklin Roosevelt was called for short
7. His mother's name

CERMAK / SIX / FIRESIDECHATS / PEARLHARBOR / POLAND

...AND AT THE SAME TIME

What was the name of the plane Wiley Post flew around the world? Winnie Mae
When did he do it? July 15, 1933

Page 31

Harry S. Truman

33rd President

Name _____

Harry Truman never went to college. He wanted to go to West Point, but his vision was too poor. He joined the state National Guard and served in France during World War I. Before becoming a U.S. senator in 1934, he had several jobs. He was elected with the help of Tom Pendergast, Party boss, but in Washington Truman exposed the Pendergast machine. Truman saved the U.S. millions when he investigated defense spending. His honesty brought him the vice presidential nomination in 1948. Eighty-three days later he was president. The war soon ended in Europe. Truman's decision to drop the atom bomb ended the war in the Pacific. He changed from a wartime to a peacetime economy. He won an upset victory in 1948. He fought against communism, for civil rights, and established NATO during his term. He did not run again, but he did remain active in politics.

Born: May 8, 1884
Birthplace: Lamar, Missouri
Political Party: Democratic
State Represented: Missouri
Term: April 12, 1945–January 20, 1953
Died: December 26, 1972
Vice President: (1) vacant
         (2) Alben Barkley (D)

DISCOVER FOR YOURSELF

Write the answer to each clue in the row of boxes to the right. There will be two words that form vertically. They will tell two things he did for recreation.

Meeting with Churchill and Stalin in 1945 — POTSDAM
First Commander of NATO — EISENHOWER
His program gave rich and poor the same — FAIRDEAL
Armed forces under one department of — DEFENSE
Past president hired to improve government efficiency — HOOVER
Struggle between communist and democratic countries (2 words) — COLDWAR
Where second bomb fell — NAGASAKI
Plan that aided war-damaged nations — MARSHALL
War U.S. entered in 1950 — KOREAN
Two things he liked _____

...AND AT THE SAME TIME

What small middle-eastern country gained independence in 1948? Israel

Page 32

Answer Key

Dwight D. Eisenhower

Name _____

34th President

Dwight Eisenhower worked in his father's creamery after high school to help pay his brother's education. Later, he went to West Point. During World War I he trained tank battalions. He had several posts between wars and had an outstanding record in all of them. He was appointed commanding chief of American forces in Europe during World War II. He was a hero after the war and was nominated for president. He won by more than any president before. As a general he had fought to win the war. As president he fought to keep the peace. He won his second term by an even greater majority. In his second term he launched the space program. But all was not peaceful. The Cold War was starting again. Castro took over Cuba, and court-ordered desegregation did not go smoothly. He was not allowed a third term by law. He retired to his farm but remained an adviser to his successors.

Born: October 14, 1890
Birthplace: Denison, Texas
Political Party: Republican
State Represented: New York
Term: January 20, 1953–January 20, 1961
Died: March 28, 1969
Vice President: Richard Nixon (R)

DISCOVER FOR YOURSELF

Write the answer to each clue in the row of boxes to the right. Rearrange the circled letters on the line below to tell what Eisenhower called his domestic program.

President of what college — C O L U M B I A

Number of Cabinet members — T E N

Wife's name (2 words) — M A M I E D O U D

Name of farm — G E T T Y S B U R G

Soviet Premier at the time — K H R U S H C H E V

Russia's space shuttle — S P U T N I K

What Eisenhower called his domestic program Modern Republicanism

...AND AT THE SAME TIME

What pitcher pitched a perfect World Series game in 1956 and for what team did he play? Don Larson, Yankees

---

John F. Kennedy

Name _____

35th President

John Kennedy came from a well-educated, prominent, Irish-American family. After college he enlisted in the Navy. He was commissioned as an ensign and commanded a PT boat. After the war he decided to run for office. His family campaigned for him. He had three terms as a representative in Congress before being elected to the U.S. Senate. He worked for aid to undeveloped countries and to end corruptions in unions. He made a name for himself and actively sought the 1960 presidential nomination four years ahead. He debated against Nixon on TV. His energetic and confident style helped him win. His attractiveness grew in the White House. He was forceful in foreign affairs. He started the Peace Corps. He supported equal rights and medical aid. He was shot after almost three years in office and did not live to see some of his legislation passed.

Born: May 29, 1917
Birthplace: Brookline, Massachusetts
Political Party: Democratic
State Represented: Massachusetts
Term: January 20, 1961– November 22, 1963
Died: November 22, 1963
Vice President: Lyndon Johnson (D)

DISCOVER FOR YOURSELF

Kennedy had a gift for speaking. He said many "catchy" things in his inaugural address. He said, "A new generation of Americans were now the leaders of government". He called his program the "New Frontier". Find what Kennedy said in his inaugural address about what you can do for your country in the puzzle to the right. Start where the arrow is pointing. Move from letter to letter in any direction without jumping a letter. Write the quotation on the lines below.

N	K	A	Y	O
T	O	S	U	T	U	R
R	W	N	A	O	C	U
Y	T	H	R	Y	O	A
C	C	O	F	O	K	S
A	U	A	D	W	H	Y
D	N	O	N	A	T	R
F	O	Y	T	C	O	N
O	R	Y	O	U	R	U

Ask not what your country can do for you. Ask what you can do for your country.

...AND AT THE SAME TIME

How many orbits did the first woman astronaut, Valentina Nikolayeva Tereshkova, make around the earth? 48

Lyndon Johnson

36th President

Name _____

Lyndon Johnson did not like to study but he made good grades. His parents had to encourage him to attend college. He began to take an interest in politics and went to work in Washington. He was in the House of Representatives over ten years. In 1948 and 1954 he was elected to the senate. He was a hard-working, persuasive legislator, but he did not convince the Party to nominate him for president in 1960. Rather he was chosen by Kennedy to be his running mate. Johnson was sworn into the presidency aboard Air Force One after Kennedy's assassination. He worked to hold the nation together and to pass some of Kennedy's legislation. He was elected to a full term in 1964. He pushed through many bills, but he also had problems. He declined to run in 1968 hoping there would be more national unity without him. He retired to his ranch in Texas.

Born: August 27, 1908
Birthplace: Stonewall, Texas
Political Party: Democratic
State Represented: Texas
Term: November 22, 1963– January 20, 1969
Died: January 22, 1973
Vice President: (1) vacant
(2) Hubert Humphrey (D)

DISCOVER FOR YOURSELF

Fill in the blanks.

His reform program was called the Great Society

He developed a long friendship with President Roosevelt

As the Senate whip it was his job to see that party members were in the Senate when a vote was taking place.

He was unpopular because of the Vietnam War.

Robert Weaver became the first black cabinet member.

His, his wife's, two daughters' and two beagles' names all had the same initials. What were they? LBJ

...AND AT THE SAME TIME

Who performed the first human heart transplant in 1967? Dr. Christiaan Barnard

---

Richard Nixon

Name _____

37th President

Richard Nixon was an outstanding student and student body leader. He began his political career almost immediately after being admitted to the bar. He enlisted in the Navy during World War II even though it was against his religion. After the war he served as a U.S. Representative and Senator where he became known for his fight against communists. He was an active vice president, but even then he was accused of misusing political donations. He had his first political defeat against Kennedy and a second for governor of California. However, eight years later he was successful in foreign affairs, but at home a cloud hung over his administration. His vice president had to resign and so did he. He retired to his California home in hopes time would take care of the hurt he caused the nation. Later, he moved back east and sometimes let his opinions be known.

Born: January 9, 1913
Birthplace: Yorba Linda, California
Political Party: Republican
State Represented: New York
Term: January 20, 1969–August 9, 1974
Died: April 22, 1994
Vice President: (1, 2) Spiro Agnew (R)
(2) Gerald Ford (R)

DISCOVER FOR YOURSELF

Find the letters that spell the answers to each clue. Cross them out in the circle as you write them after each clue. The letters that remain will spell out the name of the scandal during Nixon's term. Unscramble the letters and write the answer on the lines below.

He reduced U.S. forces here Vietnam

Two countries he visited Russia, China

Name of the dog about which he made a speech on TV Checkers

His secretary of state Kissinger

Agnew's replacement (2 words) Gerald Ford

The name of the scandal was Watergate

...AND AT THE SAME TIME

What words did Neil Armstrong speak when he stepped on the moon? That's one small step for man, one giant leap for mankind.

     IF8750 U.S. Government

Answer Key

Gerald Ford

Name _____

38th President

Gerald Ford was a good student. He studied hard and played football in high school and college. When he received his law degree, he joined the Navy. After the war he resumed his law practice. His family had always encouraged him to accept civic responsibility. He ran for the representative seat in Congress and won—the first of thirteen terms. Ford was popular among his peers, and he was influential as the minority whip. He was nominated and approved vice president after Agnew's resignation. Eight months later, he became president when Nixon resigned. The Democrat-controlled Congress and Ford had differences regarding the economy. Ford vetoed over fifty bills. He pardoned Nixon. In spite of Ford's friendly manner and strong efforts to unify the nation, the public was not consoled. He lost his bid for the presidency in 1976.

Born: July 14, 1913
Birthplace: Omaha, Nebraska
Political Party: Republican
State Represented: Michigan
Term: August 9, 1974–January 20, 1977
Died:
Vice President: Nelson Rockefeller (R)

DISCOVER FOR YOURSELF

If the answers to the clues are correct, the first letters down will spell two words.

What are they? _____

Clue	Answer
Town where Ford grew up (2 words)	G rand Rapids
His Boy Scout rank (2 words)	E agle Scout
Republican nominee in 1976	R eagan
What Ford granted draft dodgers	A mnesty
Name he was born (4 words)	L eslie Lynch King Jr.
Justice he tried to impeach	D ouglas
Job he had at Yale (2 words)	F ootball coach
Man he wrote about in 1976	O swald
His running mate (2 words)	R obert Dole
Senator he telecast with	D irksen

. . . AND AT THE SAME TIME

What was the Bicentennial? U.S. 200th birthday

James E. Carter, Jr.

Name _____

39th President

Jimmy Carter was an able student and enterprising businessman at age five when he sold peanuts. He went to the U.S. Naval Academy and was in the submarine program when his father died. He resigned from the Navy to run the family business. He was active in civic affairs, always defending those whose rights were being violated. He succeeded in becoming a state senator and governor against all odds. He authored social and moral reforms. He sought the Democratic nomination. Little known outside Georgia, he won support from the voters with his call for a return of honest government. He tried to rid the nation of economic problems, but failed. He achieved more for human rights and world peace. The public's disappointment in his inability to combat financial problems and obtain release of American hostages in Iran probably contributed to his defeat.

Born: October 1, 1924
Birthplace: Plains, Georgia
Political Party: Democratic
State Represented: Georgia
Term: January 20, 1977–January 20, 1981
Died:
Vice President: Walter Mondale (D)

DISCOVER FOR YOURSELF

What was Carter's full name? James Earl Carter Jr.

What was the family business? peanuts

Approximately, by how many popular votes did Carter beat Ford? 1,000,000

How many states did Ford win? 27 Carter win? 23

How many electoral votes did Carter win in 1976? 297 In 1980? 240

When were the Iranian hostages freed? Day of Reagan's inauguration 1/20/81

Between what two countries did Carter make peace? Egypt and Israel

In what part of the government had his mother been a volunteer? Peace Corps

. . . AND AT THE SAME TIME

What is Three Mile Island? nuclear reactor What happened there in 1979? radioactive gases escaped

---

Page 38

Ronald Reagan

Name _____

40th President

Ronald Reagan did not come from a wealthy background. He worked to help pay for his college education. He acted in school plays and was a student leader. After college he was a sportscaster before entering movies. Reagan was active in politics as a Democrat in 1948, but he became a Republican in 1962. His first public office was governor of California. He tried two times unsuccessfully to run for president before being nominated in 1980. Once elected, he set out to stop inflation, stimulate business and strengthen military defense. His critics cried loud, and his supporters defended him. He won a second term even more convincingly than the first. Terrorism rose worldwide, especially against the U.S. Reagan had proof Libya was behind much of it and ordered Libya attacked. There was criticism from around the world, but Americans stood firm behind their leader.

Born: February 6, 1911
Birthplace: Tampico, Illinois
Political Party: Republican
State Represented: California
Term: January 20, 1981–
Died:
Vice President: George Bush (R)

DISCOVER FOR YOURSELF

Write the answer to each clue in the row of boxes to the right. A word will form vertically. It will be a comet seen in the sky in 1986.

Clue	Answer
The city where the baseball team was for which he was a sportscaster	CHICAGO
The candidate of the Independent Party ticket in 1976	ANDERSON
State where he went to high school	ILLINOIS
One college major	SOCIOLOGY
Reagan's mother's name	NELLE
Age when inaugurated	SIXTY NINE
Other college major	ECONOMICS

The name of the comet is Halleys.

. . . AND AT THE SAME TIME

Who was the first citizen carried into space on January 28, 1986, and what happened? (Sharon) Christa McAuliffe, a teacher— shuttle exploded

---

Page 39

George Bush

Name _____

41st President

George Bush attended grade school in Greenwich, Connecticut, and high school in Andover, Massachusetts. Before completing his degree in economics at Yale University, Bush spent over two years as a Navy pilot during World War II, and won the Distinguished Flying Cross for heroism. After working in the oil industry, Bush became active in Republican politics. Defeated in 1964 for a seat in the U.S. Senate, Bush later became the first Republican to represent Houston in the House of Representatives. He was reelected in 1968 without opposition. Under President Nixon he served as U.S. ambassador to the United Nations, chairman of the Republican National Committee, representative to China, and director of the CIA. In 1980, he lost to Ronald Reagan in the presidential primaries. Reagan then offered him the vice-presidential nomination and Bush readily accepted. After two successful terms as Vice President, Bush was elected our 41st President.

Born: June 12, 1924
Birthplace: Milton, Massachusetts
Political Party: Republican
State Represented: Texas
Term: January 20, 1989 –
Died:
Vice President: Dan Quayle (R)

DISCOVER FOR YOURSELF

What job did Bush hold before entering politics? executive in oil industry

How many hours did Bush serve as acting-President for Reagan? approx. 8 hours

Which Vice President did Bush succeed? Walter Mondale

What is the name of Bush's wife? Barbara

To what country was Bush a liaison? China

Bush's father held what political office? U.S. Senator

Who was Bush's presidential opponent in 1988? Michael Dukakis

. . . AND AT THE SAME TIME

Which one of Neptune's moons did Voyager II take photos of? Triton

---

William Clinton

42nd President

Name _____

Bill Clinton was born in Hope, Arkansas, and named William Jefferson Blythe IV. As a teenager, he took his stepfather's name, Clinton. He graduated from Georgetown University and Yale Law School. He also spent two years at Oxford on a Rhodes scholarship. Clinton returned to Arkansas to teach law and enter public service. He was elected attorney general for the state of Arkansas in 1976 and became the governor two years later. Clinton lost his bid for re-election in 1980, but became governor again in 1982. He remained in that position until being elected President. Three issues of great interest and concern to him as governor were employment, health care and education. He has promised to continue his efforts in these areas as President. Clinton believes that the federal government should be more responsive to the needs of middle-class, working-class and poor Americans.

Born: August 19, 1946
Birthplace: Hope, Arkansas
Political Party: Democratic
State Represented: Arkansas
Term: January 20, 1993 –
Died:
Vice President: Al Gore (D)

DISCOVER FOR YOURSELF

How many years did Clinton serve as Arkansas' governor? **12.**

Name the president who served as an inspiration to Clinton while Clinton was in high school. **John Kennedy**

What was Clinton criticized for avoiding when he was a young man? **the draft**

What are the two sports Clinton engages in for relaxation and exercise? **golf   jogging**

Name the musical instrument Clinton enjoys playing. **saxophone**

At the inaugural ceremony, what well-known personality recited a poem she had been asked to compose especially for the occasion? **Maya Angelou**

... AND AT THE SAME TIME

Name the infamous leader of Iraq at the time Bill Clinton assumed office. **Saddam Hussein**

Vocabulary

Name _____

Write the number of the word on the left next to its definition on the right.

1. Electoral College
2. Plurality
3. Diplomat
4. Whip
5. Spoils system
6. Doctrine
7. Domestic
8. Gerrymandering
9. Mugwump
10. Primary
11. Levy
12. Lame duck
13. Caucus
14. Veto
15. Cabinet
16. Speaker
17. Elector
18. "Kitchen" Cabinet
19. Delegate
20. Dark horse

6 a statement of government policy
11 collection of money set by the government, a tax
9 an independent politician; in 1884, one who left the Republican Party
1 a group of electors that elect the president and vice president of the U.S.
7 carried on in one's own country
8 dividing lines of districts to give one political party the advantage
3 person who handles affairs tactfully without causing ill feeling
14 power to forbid the carrying out of a project
2 majority of votes cast for one candidate over all others
16 the officer in charge of a legislative body
18 unofficial advisers to the president who may be more important than the official group
17 one qualified vote
13 a closed meeting in which decisions are made
4 member of legislature appointed by party to enforce discipline and attendance during important sessions
12 an elected office holder continuing in office after defeat before the inauguration of a successor
20 a little known contestant for a political office
5 appointments made in exchange for favors rendered
10 an election where voters nominate their preferred party candidates (or delegates)
19 a person acting for another, a representative at a convention
15 a group of advisers to the president

How to Become a Candidate for President

Name _____

Many people from either party may want to be president. They can declare themselves as candidates and spend months campaigning before they even win their party's nomination. Once they are the party's candidate, they campaign against the other major candidate until election day.

Mark the following statements true or false.

F In order to be president a person must be over thirty-five.
T The two major parties use primaries and national conventions to select their candidates.
F Women are not allowed to run for president.
T A party platform is written at each national convention.
F A candidate for office always says the right thing to all people.
T What candidates do and say is news.
F Small party candidates are selected at the conventions.
F In order to be president a person must be a naturalized citizen.
F Primaries are held in every state.
F All delegates to the national conventions have been chosen by the voters.
F Primary elections select the president.
T New Hampshire holds the first primary.
T The two major parties hold their conventions every four years in the summer.
T The national conventions choose the presidential and vice presidential candidates.
T Delegates are chosen to go to the national conventions in the primaries.
F A favorite son is the candidate chosen by the convention.
F The candidate chosen by the party decides what the party platform will be.
T When voters choose a delegate, they are actually voting for the candidate of their choice.
T The vice presidential candidate selected at a national convention is the same party as the presidential candidate.
T No small party candidate has ever won the presidency.
F The presidential candidate may choose the vice presidential candidate without the party's approval.
T When campaigning to be the party's choice as the nominee, a person may spend years.
T When campaigning to be the people's choice for president, a person has only a little over two months to campaign.

The President's Residence

Name _____

The White House in Washington D.C. is the official residence of the president of the United States. It stands on the site selected by George Washington in 1791. The executive mansion contains the living quarters and offices for the president and his family. The White House has undergone many changes and reconstruction in its nearly 200 year history. Originally there was no plumbing or electricity. Over the years modern conveniences have come to the White House.

Write the answer to each clue in the row of boxes to the right. Two words that will form vertically is what the White House was called originally.

The room where reporters gather — **PRESSROOM**
What Dolly Madison saved of Washington — **PORTRAIT**
The largest room in the White House — **EASTROOM**
President in 1814 — **MADISON**
The floor the public may visit — **FIRST**
First White House resident — **ADAMS**
The street White House faces — **PENNSYLVANIA**
Entrance where dignitaries enter — **NORTH**
Number of rooms — **HUNDREDTHIRTYTWO**
Number of rooms when first lived in — **SIX**
Original architect — **HOBAN**
President who brought in first stove — **FILLMORE**
What British did to White House in 1814 — **BURNED**
Floor where oval office is — **SECOND**
President when Bell demonstrated phone — **HAYES**
What was the White House called originally? **President's House**

---

113   IF8750 U.S. Government

Answer Key

The Presidency

Name _____

As the chief executive of the United States, the President helps shape and enforce laws, directs foreign policy, is responsible for national defense, presides at ceremonial affairs, and leads his Party. He does not control the Legislative and Judicial Branches, but he can influence law making, and he does appoint justices to the Supreme Court. No one man can assume all the duties of the president, and so he appoints assistants. They form the White House Office. It is their job to keep the President informed about the many departments of the government. They may advise and influence the president in his decisions. The members of the White House office do not need congressional approval, nor must they answer to the Congress. The Cabinet, consisting of thirteen department heads called secretaries, is also appointed by the President to advise and assist him. However, Cabinet members must be approved by Congress and must answer to the Legislative Branch whenever asked.

Label the diagram below to show the various departments and officials running the government. Use the words from the word box to complete the diagram.

PRESIDENT	WHITE HOUSE STAFF	JUSTICES
LEGISLATIVE BRANCH	CABINET	EXECUTIVE BRANCH
SENATE	JUDICIAL BRANCH	CHIEF JUSTICE
HOUSE OF REPRESENTATIVES		SUPREME COURT

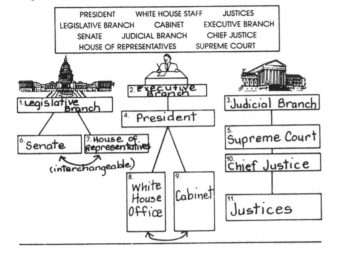

1. Legislative Branch
2. Executive Branch
3. Judicial Branch
4. President
5. Supreme Court
6. Senate
7. House of Representatives (interchangeable)
8. White House Office
9. Cabinet
10. Chief Justice
11. Justices

The Presidential Helpers

Name _____

You have learned the president has many assistants. Write the number of the White House Office division on the left of the line to its abbreviated definition on the right.

1. Council of Economic Affairs
2. Council on Environmental Quality
3. Council of Wage and Price Stability
4. Domestic Policy Staff
5. National Security Council
6. Office of Administration
7. Office of Management and Budget
8. Office of Science and Technology Policy
9. Office of the Special Representative for Trade Negotiations
10. Office of the Vice President
11. Intelligence Oversight Board
12. National Productivity Council

6 runs the White House Office, like an office manager
10 provides support to the President however needed
1 studies national economy
5 controls security
3 studies economic trends, may offer advise for controls
4 helps formulate domestic policy
2 studies national environment
12 improves productivity in private industry and government
9 works to increase trade with foreign countries
7 advises on budgetary matters
11 reports on activities of security agencies
8 advises of scientific and technological matters

There are others such as the president's physician, military aides and social secretaries that help the personal life of the presidential family run smoothly that have not been included for definition. They speak for themselves.

The White House Office often works with the Cabinet. List the thirteen departments of the cabinet and the current directors or secretaries. *Order and secretaries wil vary.*

1. Agriculture
2. Defense
3. Commerce
4. Health and Human Services
5. Education
6. Energy
7. Labor
8. State
9. Transportation
10. Treasury
11. Attorney General
12. Interior
13. Housing and Urban Development

Two Specific Powers

Name _____

Veto

Before a bill passed by Congress can be enacted as law, it must be signed by the President. Therefore, when Congress passes a bill, it sends it to him. The President has several options. He may sign it into law. He may let the bill sit on his desk for ten days, and it will become law automatically. Or, he may veto it. That is, not sign it, but return it to Congress with his objections. The President may not veto just a part of a bill. He returns the entire bill to Congress with his objections. Congress will then try to rework it or they may override the President's veto with a two-thirds veto of their own.

Fill in the blanks.

F. Roosevelt holds the record for the greatest number of bills vetoed, but was in office longer than any other president. He vetoed 635 bills. The seventeenth president, **A. Johnson**, had the largest number of vetoes overridden by Congress—15. Make a guess as to how many presidential vetoes there have been since the time of Washington. **2,385 through Carter**

Impeachment

The Constitution reads, "The President, Vice President, and all Officers of the United States shall be removed from Office on Impeachment for and conviction of Treason, Bribery, or other high crimes or misdemeanors." Impeach means to accuse. Only when an official is tried and found guilty is the official removed from office. One president has been impeached and two were close to impeachment. Can you name them from the clues?

Fill in the blanks.

This president was charged with serious misconduct in office and tried by the Senate. The trial lasted over two months, but he was acquitted by one vote. His name was **A. Johnson**.

A resolution was introduced to the House to impeach this president, but the resolution was voted down, and the president remained in office. Name him. **Tyler**

The Judiciary committee of the House recommended three articles of impeachment to the full House on this president. However, before any action could be taken, this president resigned rather than face impeachment proceedings. His name was **Nixon**.

Presidential Power

Name _____

When the president takes the Oath of Office "I do solemnly swear (or affirm) that I will faithfully execute the Office of President of the United States, and will, to the best of my ability, preserve, protect, and defend the Constitution of the United States", he accepts the responsibility of running the nation. With the responsibility comes power which could be misused. However, the authors of the Constitution tried to avoid any misuse and provided for the Legislative, Judicial and Executive Branches to be a check for one another. It has worked most of the time.

Mark the following statements true or false to see how much power the President has.

T The President is the Commander in Chief of the Armed Forces.
F The President may declare war.
T The President has the power to grant reprieves and pardons for offenses against the U.S., except in the case of impeachment.
F The President has the power to appoint any official to his Cabinet, a Supreme Court justice or an ambassador without approval from Congress.
T The War Powers Act was passed so that Congress and the President act together in declaring any act of hostility.
T The President is to keep the Congress informed with State of the Union messages from time to time.
T A treaty must receive two-thirds approval from the Senate before it is effective.
T The President may recommend legislation.
F The President may introduce legislation.
F The President may make treaties.
T The President must see that the laws are executed.
F The President does not need to consult with anyone but his Cabinet when he wants a law passed.
T The President must sign legislation in order for it to become law.
T Congress passed the National Emergencies Act in 1976 to keep the President's power in check.
F If a President does not want a law passed, he throws away the bill when Congress sends it to him.
T The President can prevent any bill from becoming law unless Congress passes it over his veto.
F The President's Cabinet and Office can pass laws.
F The President does what his advisers tell him.

---

114   IF8750 U.S. Government

Answer Key

Challenge

Name _____

How good is your memory? Name the presidents in order.

1789-1797	Washington	1885-1889	Cleveland
1797-1801	J. Adams	1889-1893	B. Harrison
1801-1809	Jefferson	1893-1897	Cleveland
1809-1817	Madison	1897-1901	McKinley
1817-1825	Monroe	1901-1909	T. Roosevelt
1825-1829	J. Q. Adams	1909-1913	Taft
1829-1837	Jackson	1913-1921	Wilson
1837-1841	Van Buren	1921-1923	Harding
1841-1841	W. H. Harrison	1923-1929	Coolidge
1841-1845	Tyler	1929-1933	Hoover
1845-1849	Polk	1933-1945	F. Roosevelt
1849-1850	Taylor	1945-1953	Truman
1850-1853	Fillmore	1953-1961	Eisenhower
1853-1857	Pierce	1961-1963	Kennedy
1857-1861	Buchanan	1963-1969	L. Johnson
1861-1865	Lincoln	1969-1974	Nixon
1865-1869	A. Johnson	1974-1977	Ford
1869-1877	Grant	1977-1981	Carter
1877-1881	Hayes	1981-1989	Reagan
1881-1881	Garfield	1989-1993	Bush
1881-1885	Arthur	1993-	Clinton

Find these other interesting facts.

Name the nine presidents who did not go to college. **Washington, Jackson, Van Buren, Taylor, Fillmore, Lincoln, A. Johnson, Truman, Cleveland**

Has your state ever sent a president to Washington? ___ If yes, name any who have come from your state. **Answers will vary.**

What profession seems to have been the one most presidents pursued before becoming president? **law** How many were in that profession? **25**

Page 49

Pairing Up

Name _____

Write the number of the president on the line next to the item it matches.

Events

1. Jefferson	7	Emancipation Proclamation	
2. Monroe	3	Watergate	
3. Nixon	9	Alaska Purchase	
4. Harding	2	Missouri Compromise	
5. McKinley	11	Social Security Act	
6. Wilson	1	Louisiana Purchase	
7. Lincoln	6	World War I	
8. Grant	4	Teapot Dome	
9. A. Johnson	10	Dred Scott Decision	
10. Buchanan	5	Spanish-American War	
11. F. Roosevelt	8	Transcontinental railroad complete	

Nicknames

1. Nixon	16	King Andrew the Great	
2. Reagan	6	Father of His Country	
3. Lincoln	14	Old Buck	
4. McKinley	5	Dude President	
5. Arthur	2	Dutch	
6. Washington	10	Father of the Constitution	
7. Eisenhower	12	Old Tip	
8. Jefferson	3	Sage of Springfield	
9. T. Roosevelt	1	Tricky Dicky	
10. Madison	8	Father of the Declaration of Independence	
12. W. H. Harrison	7	Ike	
13. J. Q. Adams	4	Wobbly Willie	
14. Buchanan	13	Old Man Eloquent	
15. A. Johnson	9	Happy Warrior	
16. Jackson	15	Tennessee Tailor	

Programs

1. F. Roosevelt	6	Manifest Destiny	5. Kennedy	4	The Fair Deal
2. L. Johnson	5	The New Frontier	6. Polk	2	The Great Society
3. Monroe	1	The New Deal	7. Wilson	3	Era of Good Feeling
4. Truman	7	The New Freedom	8. T. Roosevelt	8	The Square Deal

Page 50

Presidential Onlys

Name _____

Name the person following each "only" statement.

Only one president was sworn into office on an airplane. **Lyndon Johnson**

Only one president has been issued a patent for an invention. **Lincoln**

Only one president was inaugurated in two different cities for two different but consecutive terms. **Washington** Name the cities. **New York, Philadelphia**

Only one president had a child born in the White House. **Cleveland**

Only one president held the office of vice president and president without being elected to either. **Ford**

Only one woman was the mother of one president and the wife of another. **Abigail Adams**

He was the only bachelor president. **Buchanan**

Only one president served two full terms and yet served fifty-seven days short of eight years. **Washington** Why? **First inauguration in April**

The cause of death for one president is still a "mystery". **Harding**

He was the only president married in the White House. **Cleveland**

Only one president was a model. **Ford**

Only one president was born on a holiday. **Coolidge** What holiday? **July 4th**

Only one president resigned the office of the presidency. **Nixon**

Only one president's wife was born outside the U.S. **J. Q. Adam's**

Only one president served as speaker of the house. **Buchanan**

Only one president served two non-consecutive terms. **Cleveland**

Only one president was an actor. **Reagan**

Only one president weighed less than 100 pounds. **Madison**

Only one president has won a Pulitzer Prize for biography. **Kennedy**

Only one president married a woman whose last name was the same as his. **F. D. Roosevelt**

The only vice president that was not of the same party as the president (except at time of Civil War)? **Jefferson**

Page 51

Presidential Firsts

Name _____

Who was the first . . .

- to be nominated for vice president under the 25th Amendment? **Ford**
- president to be elected when the radio was used to give the results? **Harding**
- president on record to have his picture taken? **Buchanan**
- president elected west of the Mississippi? **Hoover** What year? **1928**
- president to appear on television? **F. Roosevelt** When? **1939**
- president to hold regular press conferences? **Wilson**
- president to be sworn in by a woman? **L. Johnson**
- president to be nominated by a national convention? **Jackson**
- president to wear long pants? **Madison**
- president to be sworn in on January 20th? **F. Roosevelt** What year? **1937**
- woman to run for the vice presidency? **Geraldine Ferraro** What year? **1984**
  - With whom did she run? **Mondale** What Party? **Democratic**
- president to live in the White House? **J. Adams**
- president to visit a foreign country while in office? **T. Roosevelt**
- president born in a log cabin? **Jackson**
- president to drive to inauguration in a car? **Harding**
- president to be sworn in behind bulletproof glass? **L. Johnson**
- president to resign? **Nixon**
- president to use the handshake rather than a bow? **Jefferson**
- mother to see her son sworn in as president? **Garfield's mother**
- president inaugurated in Washington? **Jefferson**
- president to appoint a black cabinet member? **L. Johnson**
- president to ride a train while in office? **Jackson**
- president to appoint a woman to his cabinet? **F. Roosevelt**
- president to watch a liftoff into space firsthand? **Nixon**
- president to die in office? **W. H. Harrison**
- president to marry in office (but not in the White House)? **Tyler**

Page 52

Answer Key

Presidential Quiz — Page 53

Name _____

What two presidents died on the same day? **J. Adams, Jefferson**

What is interesting about the date of their deaths? **50th anniversary of signing Declaration of Independence-July 4**

One elector wanted Washington to be the only president elected unanimously. In order to keep that record, William Plumer voted against what president? **Monroe**

Two sets of three presidents have served within one year. Name them and the year.

1. **Van Buren   W.H. Harrison   Tyler   1841**
2. **Hayes   Garfield   Arthur   1881**

What president never voted for president until he ran for the office? **Eisenhower**

What presidents were related in the following ways?

father-son **J. Adams, J.Q. Adams**   fifth cousins **The Roosevelts**

second cousins **Madison, Taylor**   grandfather-grandson **The Harrisons**

Which state has sent more presidents to Washington than any other? **NY**

Which president was the youngest when inaugurated? **T. Roosevelt** Oldest? **Reagan**

Who delivered the shortest inaugural address? **Washington**

How many words? **135**

Who delivered the longest inaugural address? **W. Harrison**

How many words? **over 8,000**

Which man gave up the presidency to the man he took it from? **B. Harrison**

How many presidents have served partial terms due to death in office? **8**

Who were the three successive presidents born in Ohio? **Grant, Hayes, Garfield**

Which presidents graduated from West Point? **Grant, Eisenhower**

Which presidents signed the Constitution? **Washington, Madison**

What three presidents' closest opponents had more popular votes, yet they won? **J.Q. Adams, Hayes, B. Harrison**

What two presidents lived to be over ninety? **Hoover, J.Q. Adams**

Which presidents' fathers signed the Declaration of Independence? **J.Q. Adams, W.H. Harrison**

Names-Faces-Places — Page 54

Name _____

Only one state is named for a president. Which one is it? **Washington**

There are four state capitals named for presidents. Name the capitals and their states. **Jefferson City, MO.   Jackson, MS   Lincoln, NB   Madison, WI**

There is one paved highway that goes from coast to coast named after a president. What is the name of the highway? **Abraham Lincoln**

What presidents' heads are on the following coins? (No fair peeking.)

penny **Lincoln**   nickel **Jefferson**   dime **F. Roosevelt**   quarter **Washington**   half dollar **Kennedy**

What presidents' heads are on the following currency? (No peeking now either.)

$1.00 **Washington** $50.00 **Grant**

$2.00 **Jefferson** $500.00 **Mckinley**

$5.00 **Lincoln** $1000.00 **Cleveland**

$20.00 **Jackson** $5000.00 **Madison**

$100,000.00 **Wilson**

What is Mount Rushmore? Describe it and tell where it is. **heads of four presidents carved in Black Hills of SD. A national Monument. (Heads of Washington, Jefferson, Lincoln, T. Roosevelt**

Tell whose president's home each of the following are and where they are located.

Hyde Park **F. Roosevelt NY**   Wheatland **Buchanan PA**

Mount Vernon **Washington VA**   Montpelier **Madison VA**

Sagamore Hill **T. Roosevelt NY**   Hermitage **Jackson TN**

Monticello **Jefferson VA**   Sherwood Forest **Tyler VA**

Spiegel Grove **Hayes OH**   The Beeches **Coolidge MA**

BEFORE THE CONSTITUTION — Page 55

Name _____

Most colonists who settled in America during its first 150 years were British. They worked hard and suffered many hardships, but they persevered as they built settlements along the country's east coast from what is now Maine to Georgia. They lived under the rule of the British.

The colonists asked for a larger role in making decisions affecting them, but the British only tightened their control. By the mid 1770's the British government had imposed heavy taxes and restricted the colonists' freedom.

On June 7, 1776, Richard Henry Lee, a delegate to the Second Continental Congress, presented the idea that the colonies should be free and independent states. As a result of his presentation, a committee was appointed to write the Declaration of Independence.

Circle the names of the thirteen colonies in the puzzle. They may be forward, backward, up, down or diagonal. Write them alphabetically on the lines to the right of the puzzle.

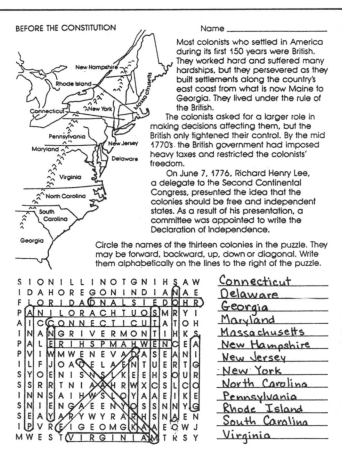

Connecticut
Delaware
Georgia
Maryland
Massachusetts
New Hampshire
New Jersey
New York
North Carolina
Pennsylvania
Rhode Island
South Carolina
Virginia

LEADING TO THE DECLARATION OF INDEPENDENCE — Page 56

Name _____

A series of events led to the writing of the Declaration of Independence. Ten years before it was written, America asked the King of England to allow it to have a more active part in making the laws that governed the nation. Their request was denied. England not only continued to make the laws, but they levied more and higher taxes. The Stamp Act required the colonists to pay taxes on legal and business papers. England also taxed many imported goods including tea. The Boston Tea Party protested the tax on tea. All but one colony agreed not to trade with England during the First Continental Congress, but England did not change its ways. A final request asking England to change was sent to King George III just before the Declaration was written.

Answer the questions and fill in the blanks below to learn which colony did not agree to stop trading with England. Its name will appear down in the boxes.

1. Write the name of the King that levied high taxes. **GEORGE**

2. How many years before the Declaration was written did America ask to be a part of the law making process? **TEN**

3. Where was a "party" held? **BOSTON**

4. Goods sent into America from another country are ____. **IMPORTED**

5. With what country did America want to share the law-making process? **ENGLAND**

6. Which Continental Congress voted not to trade with England? **FIRST**

7. What act taxed many legal and business papers? **STAMP ACT**

What state did not agree to stop trade with England? **Georgia**

Answer Key

Page 57

DECLARATION OF INDEPENDENCE

The Declaration of Independence was written after the start of the Revolutionary War. It declared America's freedom from British rule. The Second Continental Congress appointed five men, Thomas Jefferson, John Adams, Benjamin Franklin, Robert Livingston and Roger Sherman, to write it. Jefferson wrote the first draft which was almost perfect. The committee made a few corrections before it was presented to the Continental Congress. A few more corrections were made, but the document is basically the work of Jefferson. Church bells rang to signal the adoption of the Declaration of Independence on July 4, 1776—the birth of our nation.

There are five parts in the Declaration: the Preamble, Statement of Human Rights, Charges Against the King and Parliament, Statement of Separation and the Signatures. Though their main purpose was to state the reasons for separation from England, they also expressed some ideals, such as all men are created equal and entitled to the right to life, liberty and the pursuit of happiness. These ideals are also expressed in the Constitution and are the base today of America's beliefs.

Fill in the puzzle below. The circled letters when unscrambled will tell you how many people signed the Declaration of Independence.

Across
1. The main author
3. A member of the committee that wrote the Declaration

Down
1. The month in which it was completed
2. The parts in the Declaration and the number of people on the committee that wrote it.
4. 177 **S I X**, the year it was completed.

Crossword answers: JEFFERSON / LIVINGSTON / SIX

How many signers were there on the Declaration of Independence?
Fifty-six

Page 58

ARTICLES OF CONFEDERATION

During the Revolutionary War the Continental Congress wrote the Articles of Confederation that were meant to form a national government. The Articles are considered the nation's first Constitution. Under the Articles the thirteen colonies became thirteen states. The Articles granted each state its independence. The states acted like individual countries. They did not work together. They did not want to give up their individual rights. Under British rule they had, and now each state wanted its own power. The people did not want a strong central government.

The Articles of Confederation set up a Congress of the Confederation. Some states had more members than other states, but each state was allowed only one vote. There was no President, and there were no courts. Congress was limited to what it could do. The states did not have to obey the laws it did pass.

Write True or False in front of the following statements.

False The Articles of Confederation formed a strong central government.

True Every state had one vote in Congress no matter what number of delegates represented it.

False When Congress asked the states for money to pay national debts, the states did what the Congress asked.

False The President ran the Confederation.

True Every state did what it wanted.

False Every state had the same number of delegates in Congress.

False The courts helped make the laws.

True The Articles of Confederation was America's first constitution.

False Every state had to send men to serve in the army when laws were passed establishing an army.

False The President was elected by the Congress.

True The Continental Congress wrote the Articles during the Revolutionary War.

False The Articles of Confederation worked well.

Page 59

WHY THE CONSTITUTION WAS WRITTEN

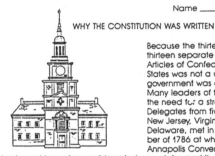

Because the thirteen states acted as thirteen separate nations under the Articles of Confederation, the United States was not a unified country, and its government was considered weak. Many leaders of the time recognized the need for a stronger government. Delegates from five states, New York, New Jersey, Virginia, Pennsylvania and Delaware, met in Annapolis in September of 1786 at what is known as the Annapolis Convention. They discussed the trade and boundary problems between states and the states' rights to do as they pleased under the laws of the Articles. From that meeting a recommendation was made that a special convention be held in Philadelphia in 1787 to revise the Articles of Confederation. Delegates from twelve states met in May of 1787. One state refused to send delegates because it was afraid it would lose its individual rights as a state. When the delegates began to discuss ways of correcting the Articles, they realized they would have to write a new document to overcome its faults. And so they worked for four months behind closed doors writing the Constitution.

Answer the questions. Unscramble the circled letters to learn which state did not come to the Constitutional Convention.

What was the name of the convention held in September, 1786?
A N N A P O L I S

In what city was the Constitution written?
P H I L A D E L P H I A

How long did it take to write the Constitution?
F O U R   M O N T H S

What kind of problems between states did the Annapolis Convention discuss?
T R A D E   A N D   B O U N D A R Y

What was the name of the state that did not attend the Constitutional Convention?
Rhode Island

Page 60

GETTING STARTED WRITING THE CONSTITUTION

George Washington had won the respect of the delegates as commander of the Revolutionary War Army and was elected President of the Constitutional Convention at its opening on May 25th in Pennsylvania's State House. As President Washington did not make many contributions, but he kept the meetings orderly and running as smoothly as possible considering the many different points of view. Any remarks Washington did make were listened to attentively by the delegates. Before the convention got underway, a rules committee organized the procedures the convention would follow. Each state was given one vote. If there were more than one representative from a state, the delegates would have to decide how to cast their one vote. What happened at the meetings was to be kept secret until the entire Constitution could be presented to the public. Any delegate could voice an opinion. A vote cast one way could be changed if the delegates saw it was necessary as they proceeded.

Complete the crossword puzzle.

Across
1. War Washington commanded army
5. Elected Washington President of convention
7. Where convention took place

Down
2. Means by which different laws settled
3. Month convention began
4. Way in which meetings held
6. Number of votes allowed per state

Crossword answers: REVOLUTIONARY / DELEGATES / STATEHOUSE

Page 57 Page 58 Page 59 Page 60

Answer Key

THE GREAT COMPROMISE

Name _____

There were several areas of disagreement. The greatest area was in the matter of how many representatives from each state should be in the legislature. The larger states thought representation should be determined by its population. This was called the Virginia Plan. The states with smaller populations were not in favor of such a plan. They wanted all states to have an equal number of representatives. Their plan was called the New Jersey Plan. Roger Sherman of Connecticut proposed a two house legislature. One, the Senate, would have an equal number of representatives. The other, the House of Representatives, would have a representative for every 30,000 residents. This plan satisfied the large and small states and became known as the Great Compromise.

Circle the answers in the puzzle and write them after each question. The letters that remain uncircled in the puzzle will spell first, the name of Virginia's governor and the name of the man who presented the Virginia Plan, and second, the man who presented the New Jersey Plan.

Which states favored the New Jersey Plan? __Small__

Representation based on population was which plan? __Virginia__

What was the first name of the man proposing the Great Compromise? __Roger__

What was his last name? __Sherman__

Which plan suggested equal representation? __New Jersey__

Which legislative body has an equal number of representatives? __Senate__

Which states favored the Virginia Plan? __large__

Which man proposed the Virginia Plan? __Edmund Randolph__

Which man proposed the New Jersey Plan? __William Paterson__

```
A I N I G R I V
E S E D M U R L
N H W D R E L A
E E J N G A D O
T R E O M L P L
A M R S H W A I
N A S L L R I A
N E N E M G P A T
S E Y E R S O N
```

Page 61

THE THREE-FIFTHS COMPROMISE

Name _____

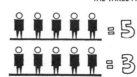

The Northern states were opposed to slavery, and the Southern states were not. The Southern states wanted their slaves counted in the population when it came to the number of congressmen that were allowed in the House of Representatives. They did not want them counted when figuring a state's taxes based on the number of its residents. The Northern states disagreed. The framers of the Constitution never used the words slave or slavery. They suggested that all free persons and three out of five of "all other persons" be counted in the population for the purposes of taxation and representation in Congress. This became known as the Three-fifths Compromise.

Give some thought to the questions below and then write your answers.
__Answers will vary. The ones below are suggestions.__

What does it mean to compromise? __A settlement of differences; a blending of thoughts from all sides__

Why were the Southern states willing to count every slave? __A larger population meant a greater representation in Congress.__

Why did the North want every slave to be counted? __The larger population of any state meant more money paid to the central government in taxes.__

Where was this compromise originally stated in the Constitution? __Article I, Section 3__

Explain how this compromise worked. __The South did not pay as high taxes as the North would have liked. However, it did not get as large a representation as it wanted.__

Do you think it was a fair compromise? _____ Why or why not? _____

Page 62

OTHER COMPROMISES

Name _____

There were other differences between large and small states, believers in a strong central government and states' righters, agricultural and industrial states, and states in different regions. They were all settled by compromise.

A. Whether to tax imported goods became an issue. The Northern states, who were becoming industrial states, wanted taxes placed on imported goods. The Southern states did not because they bought a lot of goods from Europe, including slaves. The compromise reached gave Congress the right to control interstate commerce and foreign trade, but it could not stop slave trade until 1808. A slave owner was taxed for every slave he bought because slaves were considered property.

B. Believers in a strong central government satisfied those who feared it by establishing three branches of government where no one branch could become too powerful. The Constitution provides for each branch to be checked by the other two.

C. The delegates could not decide who should elect the President and Vice-President. For this reason an Electoral College was established. Its members were to be appointed by each state legislature, and they in turn cast ballots for the two offices.

Write the letter of the compromise that governs each of the following situations after it.

The person with the most votes becomes President. __C__

Foreign goods could be higher priced. __A__

The President can veto laws made by Congress. __B__

The slave trade ended in 1808. __A__

The three branches of government are the Legislative, Executive and Judicial. __B__

Taxes on imported goods protected the Northern states. __A__

America will never have a king as head of the government. __C__

American produced goods could cost less. __A__

The Vice President receives the second most votes. __C__

The Senate must approve all treaties made by the President. __C__

Taxes are not placed on states for exported goods. __A__

No one person can make all the nation's laws. __B__

Page 63

RECORDING THE EVENTS

Name _____

James Madison is referred to as the "Father of the Constitution." He was a strong influence in its development. He spoke out more than 150 times and kept a secret record of every session that was not published until after his death.

Make believe that you were present at the time the Great Compromise was settled. Write a diary for the proceedings.

__Answers will vary.__

Write an account of how you think the proceedings happened during the debates of how citizens should be counted (the Three-fifths Compromise).

Select one of the other compromises and write about its proceedings.

Page 64

Answer Key

Page 65

SIGNING THE CONSTITUTION

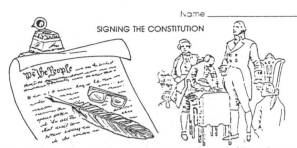

Only about thirty-five of the delegates were present for most of the entire proceedings. Seldom were all fifty-five there together. The New Hampshire delegates arrived nine weeks late. Other delegates had to leave to take care of business at home. Four delegates, Luther Martin, Robert Yates, John Lansing, Jr. and John Francis Mercer, disapproved of the Constitution and were absent for its signing. Nine delegates, Oliver Ellsworth, Caleb Strong, William Pierce, William Houston, Alexander Martin, William Richardson Davie, William Churchill Houston, George Wythe and James McClurg, approved of the Constitution but were absent at the time of its signing. John Dickinson could not be present for the signing, but he arranged for a fellow delegate to sign his name. Edmund Randolph, George Mason and Elbridge Gerry were not absent, but they did not sign the Constitution. Six delegates, Nicholas Gilman, Jared Ingersoll, Richard Bassett, John Blair, William Few and William Blount, always voted for issues when they were there, but never said a word during the proceedings.

Listed below and on the next page are the names of the fifty-five delegates to the Constitutional Convention. Circle the names of those that signed the Constitution.

New Hampshire
(John Langdon)
(Nicholas Gilman)

Massachusetts
Elbridge Gerry
(Nathaniel Gorham)
(Rufus King)
Caleb Strong

New York
Robert Yates
(Alexander Hamilton)
John Lansing, Jr.

New Jersey
(David Brearley)
William Churchill Houston
(William Paterson)
(William Livingston)
(Jonathan Dayton)

Pennsylvania
(Thomas Mifflin)
(Robert Morris)
(George Clymer)
(Jared Ingersoll)
(Thomas FitzSimons)
(James Wilson)
(Gouverneur Morris)
(Benjamin Franklin)

Page 66

Virginia
(George Washington)
Edmund Randolph
(John Blair)
(James Madison, Jr.)
George Mason
George Wythe
James McClurg

Georgia
(William Few)
(Abraham Baldwin)
William Pierce
William Houstoun

North Carolina
Alexander Martin
William Richardson Davie
(Richard Dobbs Spaight)
(William Blount)
(Hugh Williamson)

Delaware
(George Read)
(Gunning Bedford, Jr.)
(John Dickinson)
(Richard Bassett)
(Jacob Broom)

Maryland
(James McHenry)
(Daniel of St. Thomas Jenifer)
(Daniel Carroll)
John Francis Mercer
Luther Martin

South Carolina
(John Rutledge)
(Charles Pinckney)
(Charles Cotesworth Pinckney)
(Pierce Butler)

Connecticut
(William Samuel Johnson)
(Roger Sherman)
Oliver Ellsworth

How many delegates signed the Constitution? **39**
There was actually one more person that signed it. His name was William Jackson. He was secretary of the Convention. How many actual signers were there? **40**
In which states did all the delegates sign the Constitution? **Pennsylvania, Delaware, New Hampshire and South Carolina**
In which state did only one delegate sign? **New York**
How many delegates actually did not approve the Constitution? **7**
Which states had the most delegates that did not approve it? **Virginia New York**
Which state had the largest delegation? **Pennsylvania**
Which had the smallest? **New Hampshire** What did they have in common? **Both entire delegations signed.**

Page 67

FATHERS OF OUR COUNTRY

The fifty-five delegates who met in the summer of 1787 in Philadelphia had been selected by their states. They were educated, patriotic and experienced men. Over half of them were lawyers and judges, a fourth were landowners, all of them had held at least one public office, and all of them had backgrounds of some financial success. Many of the delegates were under fifty years of age. Benjamin Franklin was the oldest at 81. Though there were many differences between the delegates' ideas, they were a daring, courageous and creative group of men who were willing to take steps to establish a stronger national government. They debated, wrote and rewrote the Constitution during the summer of 1787. Although all the delegates were not always present, they had the opportunity for input into the document that is now the law of our land. Because the Constitution is the basis for our country and the product of their hard work, the men who wrote it have been named the Fathers of Our Country.

Write True or False to the following statements.

True Many of the delegates' backgrounds were similar.
False Only the men who were present all the time are the Fathers of Our Country.
True Many of the delegates were young.
False The delegates were young and inexperienced.
True The delegates disagreed on many of the ideas in the Constitution.
True No candidate was older than 81.
False The purpose of writing the Constitution was to make laws.
False Only special candidates were allowed to present ideas.
False Only one draft of the Constitution was made.
False Anyone who wanted to be a delegate could come to the Constitutional Convention.
True The Constitution presents the laws for running our country.
False Benjamin Franklin was too old to be a delegate.
False Less than fifty-five men wrote the Constitution.
True Writing the Constitution was not easy.

Page 68

READING THE CONSTITUTION

We the People

Look at a copy of the entire Constitution. It is only 4,300 words long. After you have looked at it, answer the questions or fill in the blanks below. **Some answers will vary.**

The Constitution is divided into **3** main parts.
They are the **Preamble**, **Articles** and **Amendments**
What is the purpose of the Preamble? **To introduce and explain the reasons for writing the document**
There are **7** Articles in the Constitution. Many of them have several sections. Tell which article provides for the following services or laws.
United States court system **III**
The nation's debts and upholding the Constitution **VI**
The law making body or the government **I**
What must be done for the Constitution to be law **VII**
(That process was called **ratification**.)
Explains the duties of the President **II**
Allows for changes to be made in the Constitution **V**
(That process is called **amending**.)
Tells what the states can do and what the federal government can do **IV**
There are **26** Amendments in the Constitution.
What makes the Constitution a usable document today? **The Bill of Rights and Amendments have kept it up to date.**
Which Article has allowed it to be an up-to-date document? **V**
Define the following words as they relate to the Constitution.
ARTICLE **Sections of the Constitution defining different powers**
AMENDMENT **Change in the Constitution to reflecting changing needs**
RATIFY **To pass & accept the laws proposed in the Constitution**

Answer Key

Page 69

Name _____

THREE BRANCHES OF GOVERNMENT

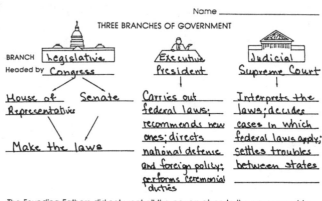

BRANCH **Legislative**   **Executive**   **Judicial**
Headed by **Congress**   **President**   **Supreme Court**

House of Representatives   **Senate**

Make the laws

Carries out federal laws; recommends new ones; directs national defense and foreign policy; performs ceremonial duties

Interprets the laws; decides cases in which federal laws apply; settles troubles between states

The Founding Fathers did not want all the powers given to the government to be controlled by one man, or even just a few men. They feared if a small group was given too much power, the United States would once again be ruled by a tyrannical government like it had been under England. To avoid such a situation they divided the new government into three branches: the executive, the legislative and the judicial. The executive branch is headed by the President of the United States who carries out federal laws and recommends new ones, directs national defense and foreign policy and performs ceremonial duties. The legislative branch is headed by Congress which consists of the House of Representatives and the Senate. Their main task is to make the laws. The judicial branch is headed by the Supreme Court. This branch interprets the laws, decides cases in which federal laws apply and settles troubles between states. The Constitution built in a "check and balance" system so that no one branch could become too powerful. Each branch is controlled by the other two in several ways. The President may veto a law passed by Congress, but Congress may override his veto with a two-thirds vote. The Senate must approve any treaty the President makes and approve many of the appointments he makes. Any money the President needs for national defense must come from the Congress. The Supreme Court may check the Congress or the President by declaring a law unconstitutional. And, the Court is appointed by the other two and may be impeached by Congress.

Label the branches of the government above and write in their Constitutional duties.

Page 70

Name _____

CHECK AND BALANCE

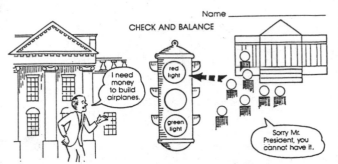

Fill in the chart below. Use the information from the preceding page.

POWER	HOW IT CAN BE CHECKED
Congress passes a law.	The President may **pass it.**
	The President may **veto it.**
	The Supreme Court may **declare the law unconstitutional.**
The President vetoes a law passed by Congress.	Congress may **override the veto with a two-thirds vote.**
The President appoints a Supreme Court judge.	The Senate may **approve or disapprove the appointment.**
A Supreme Court judge shows misconduct in office.	Congress may **impeach the judge.**
The President makes a treaty with another country.	The Senate may **approve or disapprove the treaty.**
President enforces a law.	The Supreme Court may **declare the law unconstitutional.**
The President asks for money for defense.	Congress may **give it to the President or it may not.**

Page 71

Name _____

THE HOUSE OF REPRESENTATIVES

One of the two lawmaking bodies established as the result of the Great Compromise was the House of Representatives. It is often just called the House. The Constitution provided for its members, called representatives, to be elected by eligible voters in the states. The House is also called the Lower House because it has always been the lawmaking body elected by the people every two years. This name goes back to when the common man was represented in the Lower House in England. The House is the larger of the two law-making bodies of Congress.

The Constitution states the qualifications for a representative. Look in Article I Section 2, paragraph 2 and tell what the qualifications are. **Must be at least 25 years of age, a US citizen for at least 7 years, must live in state from which chosen**

The Constitution says the members of the House of Representatives should select a Speaker from its membership to preside over its meetings. All representatives have legal immunity as members of the House. That means they are protected for anything they write or say while in office. The Constitution also stated that all representatives be paid for their service.

The Constitution gave Congress the power to determine the size of the House and to divide the representation in each state according to population, and it also provided at least one representative per state. Originally there was a representative for every 30,000 people in a state. Now there is one for about every 500,000 citizens. Six states, Alaska, Delaware, North Dakota, South Dakota, Vermont and Wyoming, have one representative today. California has the most representatives with forty-five. A census is required every ten years by the Constitution so the number of representatives may be reapportioned if necessary. When the first House met, fifty-nine members were present. At the end of the first session there were sixty-five. In 1929 legislation was passed limiting the number of representatives allowed.

Page 72

Name _____

KNOWING ABOUT THE HOUSE

Use the previous page to help you fill in the blanks below. The circled letters in the answers will spell out the number of representatives the House is limited to now.

C a l i f o r n i a has more representatives than any other state.

The number of representatives allotted per state is based on its **p o p u l a t i o n.**

A **c e n s u s** is taken every ten years to keep the population count up-to-date.

There is a representative for every **f i v e h u n d r e d   t h o u s a n d** citizens in a state.

One state allotted only one representative is **D e l a w a r e.**

The Lower House was so named in **E n g l a n d** first because it represented the common man.

There were **f i f t y - n i n e** representatives when the first House met.

Originally there was a representative for every **t h i r t y t h o u s a n d** people in a state.

W y o m i n g is allotted only one **r e p r e s e n t a t i v e.**

When the first House session ended there were **s i x t y - f i v e** representatives present.

All representatives have legal **i m m u n i t y.**

A representative must be **t w e n t y - f i v e** years old to be elected to the House of Representatives.

The number of members in the House is limited to **f o u r   h u n d r e d   t h i r t y - f i v e.**

Answer Key

Page 73

Name _____

THE SENATE

The other lawmaking body of Congress is the Senate. It is also called the Upper House. Both bodies have about the same amount of power. The Senate can introduce all types of legislation except spending bills. Only the Senate can approve or reject treaties and certain Presidential nominations for government offices.

Originally the Constitution gave each state legislature the power to select the senators from its state, but that was changed in 1913 by the 17th Amendment. Now voters in each state elect them. There is equal representation from each state in the Senate. Two senators are elected regardless of the states' population. A senator is elected every six years. No two senators are elected for six year terms at the same time from one state.

The Constitution states the qualifications for being a senator. Look at Article I, Section 3, paragraph 3 and tell what the qualifications are. __Must be__ __at least 30 years of age, a US citizen for at__ __least 9 years, must live in state from which chosen__

The only duty given the Vice President of the United States in the Constitution is that of president of the Senate. The Vice President presides over the sessions of the Senate but may only vote in case of a tie. The Senators choose a President pro tem from their membership to preside over the sessions when the Vice President cannot be there. The Constitution provides all senators legal immunity and compensation for their services.

Only twice have the qualifications of a senator been questioned. Follow the correct path to the Capitol to find out what they were.

Page 74

Name _____

MAKING LAWS

Both senators and representatives may introduce bills, but only members of the House may introduce bills that deal with taxes or spending. Both houses of Congress must pass identical versions of a bill before it can become law. Once a bill is introduced in either house, it goes through almost the same process.

When a bill is (1) introduced it is assigned to a (2) committee for consideration. If a committee does not think a bill is worthy of further consideration, it (3A) tables it. If the committee thinks otherwise, it (3B) releases it for the entire house's consideration. Most bills are often passed in the House without any opposition. But if there is some disagreement, there can be a debate. The amount of time allowed for the debate is set by its rules committee. In the Senate the rules allow a senator to speak as long as he wants. A senator may choose to filibuster to block a vote, but the Senate may vote cloture to end a filibuster or limit a debate.

When a bill is (4) passed by either house it is (5) sent to the other for its input and consideration. Any differences between either lawmaking body is worked out by a (6) joint conference committee. When (7) both houses agree, the bill is signed by the Speaker and the Vice President. Then it is (8) sent to the President for his signature.

Answer the following questions.

Who may introduce a bill? __Senators and Representatives__

What is the only exception? __Only members of the House may__ __introduce bills dealing with taxes or spending.__

What is the first thing that happens to a bill when it is introduced? __It is__ __assigned to a committee for consideration.__

If the committee does not like the bill it may table it. What does that mean? __Remove from consideration.__

Define filibuster. __A long talk to obstruct passing a bill__

Define cloture. __A vote placing a time limit on a speaker__

Who sets the time limits for debates? __The rules committee unless__ __a vote is taken in the Senate.__

Page 75

Name _____

ON TO THE PRESIDENT

Once a bill has been approved by the House and the Senate, it is sent to the President. The President may do one of several things. (9A) He may sign it and send it back to the house in which it originated, and it will become law. (9B) If he does not approve the bill, he may veto it. That is, he may return it unsigned to the house in which it originated before listing his reasons for disapproval. (B1) Congress may make changes that will meet with the President's wishes, but if it wants the bill to remain as it is, (B2) two-thirds of both houses must vote for it as is and the bill will become law in spite of the President's veto. (9C) If the President does not act on a bill sent to him by Congress within ten working days after receiving it, the bill automatically becomes law. (9D) If Congress adjourns before the ten day period is up and the President has not signed the bill, the bill does not become law.

Use the information on this page and the previous one to show the different steps and routes a bill may take. Clue: Let the numbers help you.

1. __A bill is introduced.__
2. __It is assigned to a committee for consideration.__
3A. __Table it.__   3B. __Release it for House's__ __consideration.__
4. __A bill is passed by either House.__
5. __It is sent to the other for consideration & input.__
6. __Differences are taken to a joint conference committee.__
7. __Bill is signed by Speaker and Vice President.__
8. __Sent to the President for signature.__

9A. __President signs bill and it becomes law.__   9B. __President vetoes bill.__   9C. __Bill becomes law after 10 working days if President does not act on it.__   9D. __Bill does not become law if Congress adjourns before 10 days are up.__

B1. __Congress may make changes for President's approval.__   B2. __2/3 of both Houses can override the veto.__

Page 76

Name _____

IMPEACHMENT

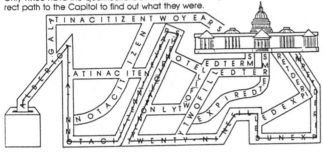

The House of Representatives has the power to impeach all government officials except members of Congress. Each house may punish its own members for disorderly behavior. Impeachment is the charge of misconduct against an official in office. A majority vote is needed by House members to bring impeachment charges against a government official. The Senate has the power to try impeachment cases. A two-thirds vote is necessary for conviction. If an official is found guilty, the official may be removed from office and never allowed to hold a United States government position again. But a conviction does not mean prison or a fine. The case would have to be tried in a regular court for that type of punishment to occur. When a President is tried, the chief justice of the Supreme Court presides. The Vice President presides over all other impeachment cases. Why do you think the Vice President does not preside over an impeachment trial if the President is being tried? __He might convict the President to become President himself.__

The House of Representatives has brought impeachment charges only twelve times. There have been only four convictions. All four were judges. One President, the 17th, was impeached for several crimes while in office. He was found guilty by thirty-five senators and acquitted by nineteen—one short of the two-thirds necessary to convict an official.

Fill in the answers below and that President's name will appear in the boxes reading down.

1. Who presides over the trial of the President? __CHIEF JUSTICE__
2. Who brings impeachment charges? __HOUSE__
3. What vote is needed for conviction? __TWO-THIRDS__
4. The House may not charge members of ___. __CONGRESS__
5. Who tries impeachment cases? __SENATE__
6. How many convictions have there been? __FOUR__
7. How many Presidents have been tried? __ONE__

Answer Key

Page 77

Name _____

COMPARING THE TWO HOUSES

Label the two houses under their pictures. Then fill in the rest of the blanks correctly.

House of Representatives _____ Senate

How can you tell?
The House is a much larger body. The Senate only has two members for each state.

What is another name for each house?
Lower House _____ Upper House

These two houses together are called **Congress**.

A member of this house is called a **Representative**	A member of this house is called a **Senator**
Age: **25 years**	Age: **30 years**
Citizenship: **7 years**	Citizenship: **9 years**
Residence: **In state that elects him/her**	Residence: **In state that elects him/her**
Length of term: **2 years**	Length of term: **6 years**
Presiding Officer: **Speaker**	Presiding Officer: **Vice President**
	Alternate: **President Pro-Tem**
Impeachment Power: **Brings charges**	Impeachment Power: **Tries person**
What vote is necessary to get impeachment? **majority**	What vote is necessary to get conviction? **two-thirds**
Introduction of Bills: **Can introduce any legislation**	Introduction of Bills: **Can introduce any legislation but money**
Passage of Bill: **Majority vote for identical bill as Senate**	Passage of Bill: **Majority vote for identical bill as House**

Members of both houses receive a **salary** for their services.
Members of both houses have **legal immunity** for anything they say or write while in office.

Page 77

Page 78

Name _____

THE EXECUTIVE BRANCH

The President heads the executive branch of the United States. In what Article of the Constitution are the duties of the President stated?
Article II

In Section 1, paragraph 1 of that Article it states the length of the President's term. What is it? **4 years** Who else is elected at the same time and for the same time period?
The Vice President

What are the three qualifications a person must have to be President? **Be a natural-born citizen, 35 years of age, 14 years a US resident**

Section 2 of the above Article states what the President's duties are. Place a check mark next to the duties given to the President by the Constitution.

___ The President may make treaties by himself.
___ The President appoints the Vice President.
✓ The President is commander in chief of the armed forces.
✓ The President makes appointments of ambassadors with the approval of the Senate.
___ The President sees that federal laws are carried out as they are designed.
___ The President does not tell Congress what he wants.
___ The President has the Congress greet visiting ambassadors.
✓ The President may make treaties with the approval of the Senate.
✓ The President commissions officers in the armed forces.

Write the oath a president must take before entering the Presidency—Article II, Section 1, paragraph 8.
"I do solemnly swear (or affirm) that I will faithfully execute the Office of the President of the United States, and will to the best of my ability, preserve, protect and defend the Constitution of the United States."

Page 78

Page 79

Name _____

THE ELECTORAL COLLEGE

The Electoral College was created by the Constitution because the Founding Fathers did not want the President elected by Congress or the people. It is a group of delegates chosen by the voters to elect the President and Vice President. On Election Day, the first Tuesday after the first Monday in November, voters mark a ballot for President and Vice President. They do not actually vote for the candidates, but they select electors, or delegates, to represent their state in the Electoral College. Each state has as many votes in the Electoral College as it has Senators and Representatives. There are 538 electors. The electors meet in December on a date set by law to cast their votes. The results are sent to the president of the Senate who opens them. A candidate must receive 270 or a majority of the electoral votes to win. After two representatives from each body of Congress have counted the Electoral votes, the results are officially announced in January. The public knows the results right after the November election because the news media figured them out. They are not official until the Electoral votes have been counted by Congress. A candidate may win the popular vote but lose the election.

Answer True or False to the following statements. The circled letters in the True answers spell out the names of two Presidents who lost the popular vote but won the election.

True The elector(a)l res(u)l(t)s are announced in January.
True The Founding Fat(h)ers did not want Congr(e)ss to select the P(r)esident.
False Each stat(e) h(a)s the same numb(e)r of electors.
True The (f)irst Tuesday after the first M(o)nday in Novembe(r) is Election (D)ay.
True Decem(b)er is w(h)en the Elector(a)l College meets.
True Voters actuall(y) vote for the d(e)legate(s).
False Congress (a)nd the public (n)ominate the candi(d)ate(s).
True A (B)allot is mark(e)d by voters in (N)ovember.
True A ma(j)ority of Elector(a)l votes (m)ake a wi(n)ner.
True (T)here (a)re five hundred thi(r)ty-eight elector(s).
False The electi(o)n for Preside(n)t is (t)he first Tu(e)sday in Decembe(r).
True It takes tw(o) hundred seventy votes to wi(n) the Presidency.

The two Presidents are Rutherford B. Hayes & Benjamin Harrison.

Page 79

Page 80

Name _____

THE JUDICIAL BRANCH

The Supreme Court heads the judicial branch of the United States government. It is the only court established by the Constitution. What Article in the Constitution states the limits of the Supreme Court? **Article III**

The Supreme Court usually makes decisions of national importance. The Court acts within the laws stated in the Constitution. Because the wording of the Constitution is sometimes hard to understand, it can be difficult to interpret the law. That is one of the duties of the Supreme Court. When the Court does make a decision, all other courts in the country must follow that decision to guarantee equal legal justice to all Americans. The Constitution also gives the Supreme Court the power to judge whether federal, state and local governments are acting within the law and also to decide if an action of the President is constitutional.

Answer the questions below. The circled letters in the answers when unscrambled will spell out what a judge in the Supreme Court is called.

The Supreme Court usually only hears what kind of cases?
N A T I O N A L

What laws guide the Supreme Court's decisions?
THE CONSTITUTION'S

The Supreme Court heads what branch of the government?
JUDICIAL

What other courts are there in the United States that must follow the decisions of the Supreme Court?
FEDERAL, STATE, LOCAL

What is a judge that sits on the Supreme Court bench called?
JUSTICE

Page 80

Answer Key

POWERS OF THE FEDERAL GOVERNMENT

The federal government in the United States divides the powers between the national government and the states. In writing the Constitution the Founding Fathers knew they had to leave enough powers with the states or the Constitution would never be approved. All states were granted the rights to control all matters relating to that state that would not interfere with other states' governments or with the national interest.

Read Section 8 of Article I in the Constitution. List the eighteen powers Congress has in your own words. Number them.

1. To set and collect taxes
2. To borrow money
3. To control and regulate commerce
4. To set rules on naturalization and bankruptcies
5. To coin money and regulate value
6. Provide punishment for counterfeiting
7. To establish post offices and post roads
8. Promote copyrighting laws
9. Establish courts under the Supreme Court
10. Punish crimes at sea
11. To declare war
12. To build an army
13. Provide a navy
14. To make government rules and regulate the army and navy
15. Allow the President to call out the militia when needed
16. Congress helps maintain state militias.
17. Congress has power over the capital and other United States possessions (forts, arsenals, etc.)
18. Allows Congress to make laws as necessary to carry out above powers

Page 81

THE RELATIONSHIP BETWEEN STATES AND THE FEDERAL GOVERNMENT

The Constitution states in Article IV the rights a citizen has in one state are the same in all the others. All states must honor the laws made in every other state, but Congress may make laws to say how those laws are carried out. This is how the Constitution attempted to keep the United States as one nation instead of separate states. This Article also states how new states may be made, and it guarantees every state its own form of government with federal help if called for by the governor.

Why do you think the rights should be the same in all states?

Answers will vary. Accept any with good reasoning.

Why should states honor each other's laws?

Congress may bring a new state into the nation, but a new state may not be made by dividing an already existing one into two states, nor can two states combine to make one state. Do you think this is a good idea? _____ Explain your answer.

Why would every state want to have its own government?

When might a governor call on the federal government for help?

Page 82

AMENDING THE CONSTITUTION

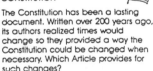

The Constitution has been a lasting document. Written over 200 years ago, its authors realized times would change so they provided a way the Constitution could be changed when necessary. Which Article provides for such changes? _____

What is a change in the Constitution called?

A change to the Constitution may be proposed when either two-thirds of Congress or two-thirds of the states request it. To be accepted as part of the Constitution, the proposed amendment must be ratified by three-fourths of the states. It is not easy to make Constitutional changes. Over 9,000 amendments have been proposed over the years, but only 26 have been ratified by three-fourths of the states. Even with popular support from the population at large, such as the Equal Rights Amendment recently had, ratification is not always assured. Currently three suggestions are being considered for Constitutional reform:

1) Change treaty ratification from two-thirds approval by the Senate to sixty percent.
2) Congress should authorize a limit to campaign spending.
3) Terms for members of the House of Representatives should be four years rather than two.

Citizens-at-large can have input into making changes by writing to their congressmen. Select one of the above. Circle the one you chose. Write a letter to a congressman telling him how you feel about the suggestion under consideration and how you would like him to vote. Back up your feelings with good reasons.

Letters will vary.

Page 83

A FEDERAL GOVERNMENT

The Constitution designed a federal government—a system which divided the powers of the national government and those of the states. In some areas the national government was in control in such things as war, treaties, trade, land matters, money and post offices. Each state controlled what went on within it, and that did not affect the nation.

Write N in front of the powers below if they are controlled by the national government. Write S if they are controlled by the states.

N A tax is placed on products coming to America from foreign countries.
S Money is given to repair state roads.
N An agreement is reached between a European country and America.
N A new stamp is designed to commemorate the signing of the Constitution.
S Speed limits on rural highways are established.
S A child must be of a certain age before entering public school.
N The borders between two states will be a river.
S The election day date for state officials was set.
N Money was alloted to build five new aircraft carriers for the United States Navy.
S Children must attend school until they reach a certain age.
N The value of money is established.
N Anyone making fake money or stamps will be punished.
N A limit was passed on the number of new immigrants allowed to come to America each year.
S Every driver of an automobile must have a license.
N There are rules for becoming an American citizen.
S A citizen will be fined for going through a stop sign.
N A government official will be tried for selling information to a foreign government.

Page 84

Answer Key

Page 85

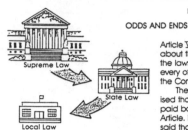

Name _____

ODDS AND ENDS

Supreme Law

State Law

Local Law

Article VI makes a few final statements about the national debt, the order of the laws in the United States, and that every official at all levels must support the Constitution.

The authors of the Constitution promised that all outstanding debts would be paid back in the first paragraph of this Article. In the second paragraph they said that federal laws were the "supreme law". That is, the Constitution, laws made by Congress, and treaties of the government were above state and local laws. The final paragraph says that officials at every level must support the Constitution of the United States first and that they never will have to take a religious test to be a government official.

The order of laws in the United States is listed below. Fill in the name of the place (city, state, town) from which they are administered. The first one will be the same for everyone. The next two will be a matter of where you live.

1. "Supreme Law" __Washington, D.C.__
2. State Laws _____ (state and capital)
3. Local Laws _____ (city or town)

Answer TRUE or FALSE to the following statements.

__True__ Every state legislator must support the United States Constitution before supporting his or her state constitution.

__True__ The United States owed money before the Constitution was written.

__False__ The Constitution's Article VI is its most important one.

__True__ The Constitution, laws made by Congress, and treaties are the highest laws in the land.

__True__ Judges in every state and city must obey the laws of the Constitution.

__False__ It is necessary to take a religious test before becoming a government official.

__True__ Article VI wraps up some details after the Constitution defined the powers of the federal and state governments.

Page 85

Page 86

Name _____

RATIFYING THE CONSTITUTION

Because the writers of the Constitution had not been given the authority by their states to write the document, it had to be sent to each state for approval. Before it could be sent to the states, it had to be written in good, easy-to-read form. The delegates asked Gouverneur Morris, an excellent writer, to write it. He did and in two days he completed its 4,300 words. On September 17, 1787, thirty-nine of the fifty-five delegates signed it and sent it to the states for ratification. Which Article in the Constitution provided the rules for its ratification? __VII__ Special conventions were held in each state to approve it. How many states needed to approve the Constitution before it could become law? __9__

People against the Constitution were afraid individual rights were not guaranteed. George Mason, Elbridge Gerry and Patrick Henry spoke out against it. Alexander Hamilton, James Madison and John Jay wrote eighty-five letters supporting its passage. They claimed the check and balance system would create a strong central government and yet preserve states' rights.

Take one side or the other and fight for or against ratification of the Constitution.

__Answers will vary.__
_____
_____
_____
_____
_____
_____
_____
_____
_____

Page 86

Page 87

Name _____

THE BILL OF RIGHTS

The delegates of the Constitutional Convention had seen no need for a bill of rights because of the limitations set on the federal government by the constitution, and because most of the states had their own bill of rights. But the citizenry felt differently. When the Constitution was sent to the states for ratification, some people would not approve it until there was a bill of rights specifically listing the individual rights of every citizen. Others ratified it with the promise there would be a bill of rights. When the first Congress met in 1789, it immediately took several amendments that had been suggested during the ratification process under consideration. James Madison wrote twelve of them which were again presented to the states for ratification. Ten were approved. They make up the Bill of Rights or the First Ten Amendments to the Constitution. Because they were written and adopted so soon after the original Constitution, they are considered a part of it.

The first amendment lists five freedoms. Circle them.

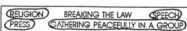

(RELIGION)   BREAKING THE LAW   (SPEECH)   HURTING OTHERS
(PRESS)   (GATHERING PEACEFULLY IN A GROUP)   TREASON   (PETITION)

Which Amendment states a search warrant is necessary before any citizen's possessions may be looked at and seized? __4__

Amendments 5 and 6 deal with citizens' rights in courts. Check the ones below that are true.

✓ No person may be tried twice for the same crime if found not guilty.

__ Anyone can be tried for a serious crime without a grand jury's indictment (a formal charge).

✓ No person must speak against himself.

__ A person may be tried without a jury.

✓ Witnesses can be a part of a person's trial.

✓ Life, liberty and property can not be taken without due process of law.

Page 87

Page 88

Name _____

MORE ABOUT THE BILL OF RIGHTS

Which other Amendment deals with jury trials? __Amendment 7__

Which Amendment provides an army for defense and the right for people to own guns for their protection? __Amendment 2__

Soldiers can live in private homes in time of war if prescribed by Congress. Otherwise they may only do so with permission of the owner. Which Amendment states this? __Amendment 3__

Read Amendment 8. What is bail? __Amount of money court requires accused to put up before being set free__

What three things does Amendment 8 forbid? __No high bail, no high fines, no cruel or unusual punishments__

The authors of the Bill of Rights could not list every individual right, so they put in the 9th and 10th Amendments to cover those not listed. What might some rights be that were not specifically listed? __Who goes to school, when cars need inspections, hunting season dates, how many dogs an individual can own, etc.__

Look at the pictures. Tell which amendment protects the pictured right. If it is not a specific right listed write 9 and 10.

__Amendment 2__

__Amendment 1__

__Amendments 9 & 10__

__Amendment 1__

__Amendments 9 & 10__

__Amendment 6__

Page 88

IF8750 U.S. Government

Answer Key

Page 89

Name _____

AMENDMENTS

Nothing is perfect—and certainly not forever. The Founding Fathers realized this when they provided for changes in the Constitution. Amendments to the Constitution have either been additions to or changes of the original document. Since the Bill of Rights was added to the Constitution in 1791, only sixteen amendments have been ratified.

Listed below on the left are the Amendments and the dates they became part of the Constitution. On the right are what the Amendments are about in a scrambled order. Read a copy of the Amendment section of the Constitution and write the Amendment's number on the line in front of its definition.

Amendment 11 (1795)
Amendment 12 (1804)
Amendment 13 (1865)
Amendment 14 (1868)
Amendment 15 (1870)
Amendment 16 (1913)
Amendment 17 (1913)
Amendment 18 (1919)
Amendment 19 (1920)
Amendment 20 (1933)
Amendment 21 (1933)
Amendment 22 (1951)
Amendment 23 (1961)
Amendment 24 (1964)
Amendment 25 (1967)
Amendment 26 (1971)

21 Repealed 18th Amendment but allowed states that wanted, to keep it.

14 Described rights of citizens, representation and voting, and defined the obligation of oath takers and Civil War debts.

24 Says no one may be kept from voting because of non-payment of a tax.

13 Did away with slavery.

26 Gave vote to citizens eighteen and older.

19 Gave women the right to vote.

22 Limited length of presidential term.

17 Changes who elects senators.

25 Provided for succession to the presidency and presidential disability.

15 Gave everyone the right to vote.

20 Changed the dates of the President and Vice President's term in office

18 Would not allow liquor to be made or sold.

23 Gave people who live in Washington, D.C. the right to vote in presidential elections.

11 Explained what kind of cases federal courts could try.

16 Established the income tax.

12 Changed how the Electoral College voted.

Page 89

Page 90

Name _____

AMENDMENT 11

Amendment 11 changes one part of Article III, Section 2 in the Constitution. Article III, Section 2 tells what cases will be heard by a federal court. Amendment 11 says that if a person from one state or a foreign country thinks he or she has something against another state, he or she can not get the case heard in any federal court.

Why do you think this Amendment was written? __Answers will vary.__

_____

What might be a circumstance where a state did something to a citizen of another state, that the citizen thought unfair? _____

_____

If a citizen of one state thought he or she had something against another state, at what level could he or she be heard? __At a state level court__

Suppose you and your family were touring in a neighboring state's capitol building and the ceiling caved in on all of you. Your father received a concussion from the falling cement and the rest of you received bad cuts and bruises. What would you do? _____

Explain how you would go about it and what you would claim? _____

_____
_____
_____
_____
_____
_____
_____

Page 90

Page 91

Name _____

AMENDMENTS 12, 20, 22 AND 25

Amendments 12, 20, 22 and 25 have something to do with the executive branch.
Amendment 12 changed Article II Section 1, paragraph 3. It was written after Thomas Jefferson and Aaron Burr tied for President, and the House of Representatives had to select a President. The electors used to vote for two candidates. They did not specify which one was for President. The one with the most votes became President and the runner-up became Vice President. Amendment 12 changed that procedure. The electors had to vote for one man for President and another for Vice President. Another change Amendment 12 made was that if no person received a majority of the electoral votes, the House of Representatives would have to elect a President from the three highest on the list. The Constitution had said it should choose from the five highest on the list.

The House of Representatives had to elect a President one other time, in 1825. Answer True or False to the following statements to find out who it was. The circled letters in the True answers will spell out that President's name.

False Amend(m)ent 12 changed the d(a)te the electors met to elec(t) a President.

True The (J)efferson-Burr tie caused Amendment 12 t(o) be written.

True The (H)ouse of Represe(n)tatives is req(u)ired to elect a Presi(d)ent when there is not a majority for one ca(n)didate.

False Aaron Bur(r) and Thomas (J)efferson shar(e)d the preside(n)cy.

False Arti(c)le I deals wit(h) the executive br(a)nch.

True Originally ele(c)tors did not have to specif(y) which candid(a)te they wanted as Presi(d)ent.

True (A)mend(m)ent(s) 12, 20, 22 and 25 deal with the Presidency.

The name of the other President elected by the House of Representatives was
__J o h n   Q u i n c y   A d a m s__.

Page 91

Page 92

Continuation of Amendments 12, 20, 22 and 25   Name _____

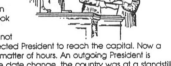

Amendment 12 referred to the fourth day of March being the starting date of the presidential term. Amendment 20, adopted almost 130 years later, changed the term of the President and Vice President to begin at noon on the twentieth day of January. This was done so there would not be such a long period of time between the election in November and when the President took office. Originally that much time was needed because transportation was not good and it took time for a newly elected President to reach the capital. Now a President can be in Washington in a matter of hours. An outgoing President is considered a "lame duck". Before the date change, the country was at a standstill the four months between the election and inauguration dates. This section is the most important part of Amendment 20.

Amendment 20 makes other changes and additions to the Constitution. The second part changes Article I, Section 4, paragraph 2 of the Constitution. It says Congress must meet at least once a year and that meeting is to begin at noon on January third. In the beginning Congress only met once a year or when the President called a special session. Now they meet almost year round. The rest of Amendment 20 explains how a President will be chosen if a President-elect dies before taking office and the procedures necessary to get Amendment 20 approved. __Answers will vary.__

Amendment 20 is often called the Lame Duck Amendment. Why do you think it is called that? __It is the most important part of the Amendment.__

What is a "lame duck" President? __One who continues to serve but has no power because he is on his way out.__

Why was there such a long period between election day and inauguration day? __It took longer to complete the count & for Presidents to reach Wash.__

Why is it different now? __We have better technology and transportation.__

What other change did Amendment 20 make to the Constitution? __The meeting day of Congress__

When did Congress meet before? __December- the first Monday__

What addition did it make to the Constitution? __How a President will be chosen if a President-elect dies before taking office__

Page 92

Answer Key

Continuation of Amendments 12, 20, 22 and 25

Amendment 22 was written after Franklin D. Roosevelt was elected to his fourth term. There had been no limit in the Constitution to the number of terms a President could serve. Until Roosevelt's time, no President had served more than two terms. Many felt this was too long a time for one person to serve and so the twenty-second Amendment was written. Amendment 22 states that no person may be elected more than twice, and that anyone who has been President for more than two years of someone else's term cannot be elected more than once.

Amendment 25 changes and expands Article II, Section 1. It came about when Lyndon Johnson moved into the Presidency after John Kennedy was assassinated and there was no Vice President for almost fourteen months. Amendment 25 says when there is no Vice President the President should nominate one, and if half the Senate and House of Representatives vote in favor of the nomination, that person will be the Vice President. Death had been the only way a President had vacated the office until 1974. In 1974 President Nixon resigned. Gerald Ford, who had been appointed Vice President when the vice presidency was vacated earlier, took over the office of President. With the vice presidency again vacated, President Ford nominated Nelson Rockefeller for Vice President. The amendment worked. Amendment 25 also provides for the Vice President to take over the President's duties when the President is unable to perform his job. This part of the amendment proved it worked too. When President Reagan had surgery in 1985, Vice President Bush assumed the presidency for eight hours.

Why was Amendment 22 written? _Lyndon Johnson created a vacancy*_
in the Vice Presidency. People worried about the open slot.

What is the most number of years a President could serve? ___10___

If a President can only be elected to two terms, then explain how he could serve that number of years. _If he served out two years or less of_
another President's term, and then was elected
to two terms.

* Answers could vary.

Continuation of Amendments 12, 20, 22 and 25

Tell under what circumstances the following were President.

Gerald Ford __Nixon resigned.__
George Bush __Acting President when Reagan had surgery__
Franklin Roosevelt __Elected four times__
Lyndon Johnson __After Kennedy was shot__
Richard Nixon __Elected two times__

Review of the Presidential Amendments

Give a title to each of the Presidential Amendments

Amendment 12 __Electing a President and Vice President__
Amendment 20 __Lame Duck__
Amendment 22 __Length of Service__
Amendment 25 __Presidential Succession and Disability__

Which amendment was written after there was a tie for the presidency? __12__

Which one was partially written to see that the government was always run by an able person? __25__

Which amendment was written to limit a President's length of service? __22__

Which one redesigned how the President and Vice President were elected? __12__

Which amendment changed the date the President took office? __20__

Answer True or False to the following statements.

__False__ A presidency is only vacated upon the President's death.

__True__ Electors must specify one candidate for President and another for Vice President.

__False__ A lame duck President is disabled.

__False__ No President has ever held the office longer than ten years.

__True__ One President acted as President for only eight hours.

__False__ If the electors fail to give one candidate a majority of the votes for President, the Senate elects a President from one of the three highest vote getters.

__True__ When Lyndon Johnson left the vice presidency to become President, there was no Vice President.

__True__ Gerald Ford was not elected President.

__True__ A person who has been President for more than two years of someone else's term cannot be elected more than once.

AMENDMENTS 13, 14 AND 15

Amendments 13, 14 and 15 are often called the Civil Rights Amendments. The Founding Fathers had so many disagreements about the treatment of slaves, that there almost was no Constitution. Slavery by name was not mentioned in the Constitution. Not until after the Civil War was slavery abolished. Amendment 13 gave black people their freedom.

The first section of Amendment 14 made black people citizens and entitled to the same rights guaranteed all citizens by the Constitution. Section 2 of this amendment changed Article 1, Section 2 of the Constitution. Every black is now counted as one person instead of three-fifths of a person. This section also imposes a penalty on any state that refuses to let all male citizens, twenty-one or over, vote. The rest of Amendment 14 controlled the positions federal officers who had joined the Confederacy might have and payment of the Union's Civil War debt.

Amendment 14 does give all adult males that are citizens the right to vote. Amendment 15 carries it a step further and states that no citizen may be kept from voting because of race, color or previous condition of servitude (slavery).

Solve the crossword.

Across
1. What was fought between the states?
3. Word not mentioned in the Constitution.
4. What Amendment 13 gave all black people.
6. The amendment that made blacks citizens.

Down
1. What Amendments 13, 14 and 15 are often called.
2. No citizen can be kept from voting because of this.
5. Every black is now counted as ___ person.

Crossword solution:
- CIVILWAR
- SLAVERY
- FREEDOM
- FOURTEEN

AMENDMENT 16

Amendment 16 gives Congress the right to tax individuals according to the amount of money they earn. It was first proposed as an amendment in 1894, but it was ruled unconstitutional by the Supreme Court. It became part of the Constitution in 1913. Until then the only way Congress got money to pay debts and provide the necessary defense for the country was through taxing imported items, and on items made, sold and used in the United States. Such taxes were the same in all the states. The income tax created by Amendment 16 raised much more money. When the amendment became law, a part of every person's salary was taken out for taxes. It was thought to be a fair tax because it was a way to give the government money for running the country according to each individual's ability to pay. More people probably complain more about Amendment 16 than any other amendment.

Do you think Amendment 16, the Income Tax Amendment, is a fair one? _____
Explain your answer. _____ Answers will vary. _____
_____
_____
_____

Think of some ways the government spends the money received from individuals' incomes. _____
_____

Why do you think people complain about Amendment 16? _____

Take a poll. Ask several working people if they think paying an income tax is necessary, if it is fair, and if they can suggest other ways for the government to raise money.

#	NECESSARY?	FAIR?	OTHER WAYS
1			
2			
3			
4			

(Use back of page if necessary.)

Answer Key

Page 97

Name _____

AMENDMENTS 18 AND 21

Amendment 18 is called the Prohibition Amendment. This amendment made it illegal to make, sell or ship any alcoholic beverages anywhere in the United States. It also prohibited exporting them out of or importing them into the country. Businesses that made or sold liquor had one year from the time Amendment 18 was passed to stop making it. A time limit of seven years for ratification was placed on this amendment. Since then, most amendments have given a seven year time limit from the time of proposal to ratification. One year after this amendment was ratified it became law. Fourteen years later Amendment 18 was repealed by Amendment 21. Amendment 21 withdrew the federal limitations on the manufacturing and selling of alcoholic beverages, but recognized the rights of individual states to still practice prohibition.

Define prohibition. _To forbid by law the making & selling of liquor_

Define repeal. _Cancel, take back, revoke_

Do you think a seven year limit for ratification is a good idea? ____ Why or why not?
Answers will vary.

Why did it take one year after ratification for Amendment 18 to become effective?
Businesses had to stop making liquor and get rid of their stock.

Did Amendment 21 make prohibition illegal? _No_ Explain your answer. _States had the right to continue prohibition if they wanted._

Do you think laws should be made because they are best for the country or because they are strong personal beliefs and morals? _Answers will vary._
Explain your answer. _____

Page 98

Name _____

AMENDMENTS 17, 19, 23, 24 AND 26

Amendments 17, 19, 23, 24 and 26 all have something to do with voting. They either changed parts or expanded the Constitution. Amendment 17 changed Article I, Section 3 of the Constitution. Amendment 17 gives the people the right to elect their senators. The 17th Amendment also directed the governor of a state to choose a vacated senatorial seat until the election could be held.

How were senators elected before Amendment 17? _By their state legislatures_ because the authors of the Constitution thought the general public would not be well enough informed to make the right choice.

How were vacancies filled before Amendment 17? _Governor made temporary appointment until state legislature could._

Amendment 19 gave women the right to vote. This cancelled a part of Amendment 14. Explain how it did that. _Amendment 14 referred to male voters._

People living in the District of Columbia, the United States Capital, could not vote in Presidential elections because it was not a state. Amendment 23 gave them that right. Now the Capital has one elector that meets with the electors from all the states to elect the President and Vice President.

Why didn't the people in the country's capital vote for President before Amendment 23 became effective? _It was not a state._

Amendment 24 ruled that no United States citizens could be kept from voting in a federal election because they had failed to pay taxes. Some states tried to keep some people from voting if they had not paid their taxes. Why do you think some states tried this? _To keep the poor and/or blacks from voting_

Amendment 26 changed the age at which people could vote to 18. Although the Constitution said the age at which people could vote should be set by the states, one amendment stated the age. Which amendment was it and what age did it state? _Amendment 14 - 21_

Page 99

Name _____

KNOW YOUR CONSTITUTION!

Circle the correct answer to each of the following questions.

How many delegates signed the Constitution?   50   40   (39)   44   55

Which amendments are sometimes referred to as the Civil Rights Amendments?
11, 12, 13   12, 13, 14   (13, 14, 15)   14, 15, 16

What had to be done to ratify the Constitution?
A Bill of Rights had to be written.
The delegates had to sign it.
Eighty-five letters written to support it.
(Nine states had to approve it.)

Who was not a delegate, but signed the Constitution?
(William Jackson)   Benjamin Franklin   George Mason
Edmund Randolph   Gouverneur Morris

Which state did not attend the Constitutional Convention?
Delaware   Georgia   New Hampshire   (Rhode Island)

Who was considered "Father of the Constitution?"
George Washington   (James Madison)   Benjamin Franklin
Roger Sherman   Alexander Hamilton

Which part of the Constitution has seven parts?
Bill of Rights   Amendments   (Articles)   Preamble

Who may introduce all kinds of bills?
The Supreme Court   (The House of Representatives)   The Senate
Lobbyists   Citizens   The President

Who can veto a bill?
A senator   A justice   (The President)   A representative

What document did the Constitution replace?
Declaration of Independence   (Articles of Confederation)
Bill of Rights   Federalist Papers

Which compromise is referred to as the Great Compromise?
(Two house legislature)   Establishment of the Electoral College
Slave 3/5 a person   Establishment of three branches
Congress controlled interstate commerce and foreign trade.

Who is president of the Senate?
The majority leader   The Chief Justice   The President
The president pro tem   (The Vice President)

Who hears impeachment charges against a government official?
(The Senate)   The Supreme Court   The Executive Branch
The House of Representatives

Page 100

Name _____

MATCHING CONSTITUTIONAL FACTS

Write the letter in front of the fact or event on the left on the line to the right that goes with it.

A. This state refused to stop trading with England.
B. The Declaration of Independence
C. Five states came to the meeting.
D. Women given right to vote
E. City where Constitutional Convention held
F. It was abolished with Amendment 13.
G. Every state is given two.
H. Enforces the law
I. Check and balance system
J. The Virginia Plan
K. Needs to be thirty years old and a citizen for 9 years
L. Introduces all bills having to do with money
M. Signed the Declaration of Independence, the Articles of Confederation and the Constitution
N. The people do not like it.
O. Events were kept secret.
P. Describes the Legislature
Q. Have made the Constitution a lasting document
R. There are 9 of them.
S. Interprets the law
T. It elects the President and Vice President.
U. Assigned to a committee for consideration
V. Became Presidents of the United States
W. One of first things the first Congress did

K _A senator to be elected_
V _George Washington and James Madison_
H _Executive Branch_
N _The Income Tax Amendment_
B _Adoption July 4, 1776_
L _House of Representatives_
P _Article 1_
C _Annapolis Convention_
J _Called for representation according to population_
Q _Amendments_
A _Georgia_
G _Senators_
M _Robert Morris and Roger Sherman_
F _Slavery_
U _A bill that has been introduced_
R _Supreme Court justices_
D _Amendment 19_
S _Judicial Branch_
I _Three branches in the government_
E _Philadelphia_
W _Wrote the Bill of Rights_
T _Electoral College_
O _Constitutional Convention_

Answer Key

MATCH THE ACTS WITH THE MAN!

Name _____

The names of the men listed in alphabetical order on the left were all participants in the Constitutional Convention. The numbers after their names tell on what page some information may be found about them. Use these and the documents themselves to write the letter next to each fact on the line in front of each man's name if it describes that man. Some men will have more than one fact true about them.

C	George Clymer	
D	Jonathan Dayton	
H	John Dickinson	
C,F	Benjamin Franklin 11	
P	Elbridge Gerry 34	
L	Alexander Hamilton 34	
A	William Jackson	
I,J,L,O	James Madison 10, 34	
P	George Mason 34	
B	Gouverneur Morris 34	
C	Robert Morris	
K	William Paterson 7	
C,Q	George Read	
N,R	Edmund Rudolph	
C,G,M	Roger Sherman	
E,J	George Washington 6	
C	James Wilson	

A. Secretary of the Convention
B. Actually wrote the words of the Constitution
C. Signed the Declaration of Independence
D. Youngest delegate at the Convention; was last in New Jersey delegation to sign the Constitution
E. President of the Convention
F. Oldest delegate at the Convention
G. A delegate from Connecticut and Robert Morris signed the Constitution, Declaration of Independence and the Articles of Confederation
H. Had another delegate from Delaware sign for him
I. Kept secret records of every session
J. Became President of the U.S.
K. Presented the New Jersey Plan
L. Authored several letters supporting ratification of Constitution
M. Suggested there be two lawmaking bodies in Congress
N. Presented the Virginia Plan
O. "Father of the Constitution"
P. Spoke out against ratification of Constitution because it did not guarantee individual rights
Q. Signed Constitution twice—once under his name; once under the name of another delegate
R. Virginia's Governor; did not sign Constitution

Page 101

CONSTITUTIONAL VOCABULARY

Name _____

Write the definitions for the following words as they relate to the Constitution of the United States.

ABOLISH Get rid of, do away with
AMENDMENT A change or addition to the Constitution
BALLOT A printed list of candidates on which to make a choice
BILL A proposed law going through lawmaking process
CENSUS Count of people
CHIEF JUSTICE Head judge of Supreme Court
CIVIL RIGHTS Any rights to do with the people
COMPROMISE A way to settle differences
DELEGATE An appointed representative of the people
DUE PROCESS Complete and fair working of the law
ELECTOR A person who elects, member of electoral college
FEDERAL Anything to do with central government
IMPEACH Accuse government official of misconduct in office.
LAME DUCK Government official still in office but not re-elected
LEGISLATURE Lawmaking body
MAJORITY More than 50 percent
PETITION An appeal or plea
PREAMBLE Introduction to Constitution
PRESIDENT PRO TEM President of Senate when VP is absent
QUORUM Necessary number of people to do business
RATIFY Approve
REAPPORTION To divide up again
SEIZURE Grabbing by force
TREASON Doing something against one's government
VETO Power to stop something from happening

Page 102

About the book . . .

This book provides a unique and interesting approach that goes beyond the traditional naming of our presidents, to understanding the Presidency and learning about those who have held the office. One page is devoted to each president with additional pages designed to explain the functions and significance of the office.

The activities dealing with the Constitution were designed to help students develop an overall knowledge of this important document. The pages are self-contained and are also useful in affording students practice in reading comprehension.

About the author . . .

Claire Norman is an experienced author and veteran teacher, with a Master's Degree in Reading and an Advanced Graduate Certificate from Washington University. She is well prepared to develop materials for children and her 33 years of teaching experience include all of the elementary grades, remedial reading and the teaching of art.

Credits . . .

Author: Claire Norman
Editor: Lee Quackenbush
Artists: Pat Biggs and Ann Stein
Production: Pat Geasler
Cover Photo: Frank Pieroni

Special thanks to David Lemmink for allowing us to use a portion of his political button collection for our cover photo.